SETTING LEADERS

The Island Life of the Last East Coast Ocean Pound Trap Fishermen

RON SCHAPER

Copyright © 2023 Ron Schaper

All rights reserved. No part of this publication in print or in electronic format may be reproduced, stored in a retrieval system, or transmitted in any form or by any means, electronic, mechanical, photocopying, recording, or otherwise without the prior written permission of the publisher.

The scanning, uploading, and distribution of this book without permission is a theft of the author's intellectual property. Thank you for your support of the author's rights.

Editing by Andrea Dowling
Design and distribution by Bublish

ISBN: 978-1-647045-20-3 (paperback)
ISBN: 978-1-647045-21-0 (hardcover)

*Dedicated to my mom and dad, Mary and Louis Schaper,
who made all of this possible.*

Give a man a fish and you feed him for a day;
teach a man to fish and you feed him for a lifetime.

Foreword

Written by my mom, Mary Schaper, who lived it.

Sunrise Fish Company

The Sunrise Fish Company, as well as the Short Beach and the Long Island Fish Companies, were originally situated on the south side of Oak Beach across from the Fire Island Coast Guard Station. In 1935, the State Boat Channel was being dredged and the sand was thrown to the north side of the channel, thus creating a new sand island. Robert Moses made the decision to relocate the commercial fish companies from Oak Beach to this new island so that the beach road from Jones Beach could extend eastward to what is now Captree State Park and Boat Basin. The new island would be named Havemeyer Point Island, known as Fishermen's Island to the locals.

The fishermen built large boardwalks on their section of land which had been divided into distinct Fish Company areas. Sunrise Fish Company was deeded the most southern part of the new island with Short Beach and the Long Island Fish Company of West Sayville the second and third section. Many of the equipment sheds were transported across by boat to the new Fishermen's Island and several summer family homes were built by the fishermen at a time when they only came to their mainland homes on Wednesday nights and weekends. At that time there weren't any bridges that crossed the bay and families were more isolated. Each fishing company had a "cookhouse" with a hired cook who provided all the fishermen's meals. The cook lived there the entire season. The fishermen slept in bunk houses, two or three to a house, ate all their meals in the cookhouse, and could go to the mainland on weekends if they had a family locally. Fishermen were up by 6 a.m., had breakfast in the cookhouse and set out for their nets by 6:30.

Sunrise Fish Company had four nets in 1942. The fishermen returned from the ocean around noon, depending on the weather and the catches. The cook had a hot meal ready for them after which the pound boat crossed the bay to unload and pack their catch on the mainland. If there was a boatload of fish all the crew was needed inshore where they packed the fish and iced it up before crossing the bay again for a fish supper by the cook and then an early bedtime.

If the catch was light some of the crew stayed on the dock to repair nets, dip them in copper paint and prepare them for when they were needed. Nets were changed about every 4 to 5 weeks depending on weather conditions and the amount of sea growth they collected.

Fishermen worked Monday through Friday, 6 a.m. to about 6 p.m. and a so called 1/2 day on Saturday; that is, they worked until the fish were unpacked, iced up and put in storage and the fish boat was scrubbed down. They all hoped for a light catch on Saturdays!

Upkeep of equipment on the boats - the sharpies, the scow and pound boat, plus the constant care and repair of the net sheds and boardwalk kept the fishermen busy constantly. The houses were originally lighted with kerosene lamps until later when a generator house was built. The generators were maintained daily and used to provide electricity only as needed. Their main use was to power the water pump and to provide electricity for the wringer washer machines that were used in the 1950s and 1960s for the fishermen's families.

We did have gas stoves and some had hot water tanks heated by propane. The pound boat brought ice for the iceboxes several times a week to keep food cool until the era of gas refrigeration came in. Families with iceboxes used their perishable meats and vegetables first, then relied on fish catches which came in daily.

Children of the fishermen who lived at the beach loved the island way of life and never wanted to go ashore. They swam and clammed and rowed. They visited kids on the other islands, and never tired of playing in the sand, the water and in the net sheds. They put on skits for their families. The big event of the day was when the pound boat was seen coming around the bend from the inlet. The children would announce its coming and all would go down the dock to meet it and see the catch of the day.

When the children were small, bedtime was when the lighthouse came on. When they were older, parents tried to keep their eyes on their teenagers and herd them in after dark for safety and rest ... so many out of the way places to meet and date!

Life at the beach was, and remains today, a rustic and meaningful lifestyle; a simple time set aside from the many pressures of modern life.

Family members of the original fishermen who labored long and hard in their generation have endowed their children's families with the same deep regard and appreciation of the past; the fishing industry, the historic lifestyle, the beach life as it was then lived.

It is those families who now occupy those fishermen's beach houses who have a fervent desire to preserve the past. It is their heritage and their dream to carry this meaningful life on for themselves and future generations - a way of life which sometimes seems as fleeting as the sands along the shoreline.

Written by Mary Schaper,
Wife of Captain Louis Schaper of the
Sunrise Fish Company
Degnon Boulevard
Islip, New York 11751

SETTING LEADERS

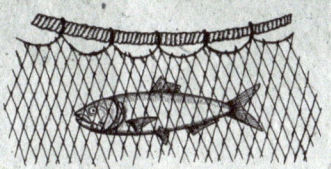

Son of a Fisherman

The stiff wire handles of the wooden bushel basket dug deep into the soft hands of the 8-year-old schoolboy. Even though he carefully selected the lighter bedroom baskets loaded with bed linens, towels, blankets and clothing, they were still a bit much to carry through the house to the garage, where his older brothers were packing them into the Ford station wagon. He left the much heavier kitchen baskets, which held Mom's cast iron frying pans, sauce pans and casseroles, for them to carry together, one on each handle. There were numerous baskets of kitchen utensils and canisters of flour and sugar, wooden rolling pins, and other necessities. These covered round wooden baskets were meant to hold a measured bushel of clams or blue claw crabs. But these new clean ones Dad pressed into service for the family goods.

This twice a year migration was a lot of work and lugging, but as a kid, there was excitement in the air; we were moving to the beach!

Memorial Day marked the season's first trip to the beach house. After the Babylon Village Memorial Day parade, marching with Cub and later Boy Scouts, watching Mr. Stecker adorned with his volunteer fire department dress blue uniform, polished fire hook over his shoulder, marching with the sparkling red fire trucks, then scrambling with the kids at the park for the spent rifle cartridges from the 21-gun salute, we rushed home to begin loading the first truckload of gear for the beach.

Dad's pickup truck and the family station wagon were packed with the bushel baskets, boxes, Dad's old Navy duffle bags, laundry baskets and bundles of towels and linens. Prior to the completion of the Captree Bridge in 1954, we loaded all of this gear onto the Sunrise Fish Company's pound boat in Islip for the trip across the Great South Bay to the island. Dad would cover the small mountain of household goods with heavy canvas tarps to protect it from any spray or rain. After the bridge was built, we would drive over to Captree Boat Basin where the skiff was moored and was loaded up for the short trip across the State Boat Channel to the island. (The skiff was a launch used by the fish company to shuttle back and forth between Captree and the island; it is further described below.)

Since sadly leaving the island for school at the end of last summer, we were eager to scurry around to check out everything. But first we all had to pitch in and lug the packed household goods up to the beach house at the other end of the boardwalk. The two old wooden wheelbarrows with iron wheels were loaded down with some of the heavier items. With a squeaking bump, bump sound over the dock planks, they would traverse the big dock. On the narrow 4 plank wide "skinny" boardwalk that started at Uncle Arie's house, the wheelbarrow would only bump every 8 feet or so where the planks were joined. The iron wheel was narrow so care had to be taken so that it didn't jam between the boards and dump the load into the reeds and poison ivy which lined the sides of the walk.

Setting Leaders

The wheelbarrows were just like this one.

The original beach house showing the typical "skinny boardwalk."

By the end of the first week of summer, our bare feet knew each one of the planks in the boardwalk. We learned which boards to avoid because they were splintery or had tar on them, or were a dark color that got hot in the sun. Walking down the boardwalk—or often running—our feet would automatically shift from one side of the walk to the other to land on the preferred planks.

After numerous trips back and forth between the skiff and the house, the mountain of gear was heaped on the floor. The work was just beginning for Mom and Dad who had to stow all of this stuff. For us kids—we had our own agenda. First, we checked out our boats. For the winter, these were tipped up on their sides or upside down on blocks of wood in the sand behind the big net shed. We did a quick look to size up what work would be needed to get the boats ready for the water. There was no time to get started right now—there were too many other things to check on since leaving the beach nine months earlier.

We always took a walk around the island, noting the high-water marks from winter storms and to see how much erosion had taken place, slowly reducing the size of the island, bringing the houses even more perilously close to the lapping waves of the Great South Bay. Abandoned duck hunters' blinds would yield empty shotgun shells. Sometimes we found treasures in mounds of collected seaweed: fishing lures and dobbers, various fishermen's hats, a lost life ring, or even an occasional bottle with a note inside.

Then back to our bedrooms or bunk house to dig through a musty smelling dresser for one of many bathing suits from last season. This was only late May in New York, so the water temperature was still very chilly. It didn't matter—it was Memorial Day and we were finally back to the beach. We were going swimming! Brrrrrr … it was cold! But we always went in … looking forward to the warmer days ahead.

After rummaging through our toy boats, mildewed classic comic book collection, then checking out the net sheds and scow, Mom and Dad usually had a few more chores for us before we had to head back home to the mainland. We had two more weeks of school before we could move to the beach for the summer … and we couldn't wait.

When we finally came racing out of school with our report cards it was at last time to finish packing up for the move to the beach—this time for the whole summer! A lot of the gear had been moved over on Memorial Day, but now there were more things that were used every day and tons of food. We were eager and willing to work to help get our family over to the beach and let the summer begin.

Spending the first night of the summer at the beach house always had a certain magic about it. The familiar bed and room were the same as before, but it still felt somehow foreign and different … so very unlike my bedroom on the mainland. Lying in bed awake, getting reacquainted with the beach sounds; the breeze brushing the reeds against the house, the putter of a motorboat heading home in the dark followed a bit later by the crash of its waves washing on the shore, the squawk of a gull, chirping of crickets, and the regular 7½ second flash on the wall from the Fire Island Lighthouse. The easterly facing bedroom window blasted the morning sun in for an early start of the day. The first item on the agenda at the beginning of our summer was to get the boats ready. As the years progressed, we had quite a collection of boats.

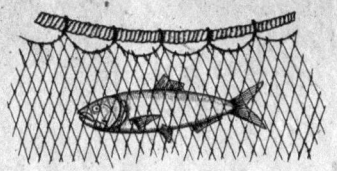

Our Boats

"Believe me, my young friend, there is nothing - absolutely nothing - half so much worth doing as simply messing about in boats."

Kenneth Grahame, The Wind in the Willows

Just as Eskimos have many words for snow, we were familiar with so many types of watercraft that to just say "boat," wasn't enough information. Even the youngest kids knew the difference between a skiff, a garvey, the pom boat (pound boat), the scow, a Beetle Cat, pram, and a sharpie. Also in our world were party boats, ferries, Coast Guard boats and an occasional tanker.

Sharpies

My brothers and I started by sharing a sharpie rowboat. These were typically about ten or twelve feet long, 4 feet wide and 16 inches deep. There was a small narrow seat in the bow, two seats in the middle, each fitted with oar locks, and a broad seat in the stern.

Our sharpie was similar to this, but without the fancy varnish finish.

The bottom was what is called "cross-planked," which means it leaked! Actually, the bottom had numerous seams between the planks which were traditionally caulked with cotton. When the boat was out of the water for the winter, the wooden boards would dry out and shrink. You could see daylight through the seams when looking from underneath! Usually, we gave all of the boat's surfaces a cursory scraping to remove any loose, peeling paint. Then we painted it inside and out with whatever paint we found in the machine shop. We painted the bottom with oil-based red copper paint and after it dried in a day or so, we moved the boat on rollers down to the water to launch it.

Immediately water bubbled up through the seams, then settled to equilibrium and the boat floated with about 6 inches of water inside. Bailing it out now proved useless as water just kept coming in. It took 3 or 4 days for the dry wood to swell up enough to only require bailing once or twice a day. If a seam leaked too badly, we hauled it back out, turned it over and Dad re-caulked the seam with fresh cotton. Bailing out wooden sharpies was just part of their nature.

But these were perfect boats for kids. Like all sharpies, their flat bottom gave them great stability. They were easy to row, they could hold a whole gang of kids safely, the shallow draft was perfect for the flats and meadows, and there was room to carry bushel baskets for clams and crabs, nets, eel spears, fishing poles and oars. They could be rowed by one person, or any number up to four.

My favorite spot was sitting on the bow facing aft. At the age of 5, I happily enjoyed riding there as Richard rowed from the middle seat and Bob sat back aft. Once, without warning, Richard suddenly backed the oars, stopped the boat ... and sent me flipping backwards over the bow into the water! My mom watched horrified from her seat on the jetty. I hadn't yet learned how to swim! So still wearing her new non-waterproof wristwatch and fully clothed, she jumped in to save me ... while I calmly dog paddled myself to the shallow water. I guess I could swim after all!

Sailing Dinghy (Pram)

While we had lots of fun with the big clunky sharpie, one winter Dad surprised us when he got plans for a sailing dinghy. Working nights in his basement workshop, he cut panels of marine plywood and formed and shaped oak strips for the gunwales, frames, bilge strakes and breast hooks. Soon the 8-foot pram took shape with a small centerboard trunk, mast step up forward, and a gudgeon and pintle hung rudder on the transom.

Dad was only too familiar with the leaky habits of wooden boats and he was aware of the new material called fiberglass and its promises of making wooden boat seams impervious to water. He bought rolls of 4-inch-wide fiberglass cloth and a can of polyester resin with the little bottle of hardener, and the recommended acetone and brushes to do the job. There was some fine print on the can—something about working in "a well-ventilated area." Hey, it was winter in New York, so maybe he propped open a cellar window. But the pervasive smell of styrene wafted up through the wooden floors and up the cellar stairs. However it got there, the entire house was flooded with the eye-stinging, throat-burning stench of a fiberglass boat factory. One unfortunate discovery was that the butter in the kitchen had absorbed the styrene fumes to such an extent that any sandwich or food made with that butter tasted like a chemical poison. That was Dad's first experiment with fiberglassing ... in the house.

The fiberglass set up well. The next discovery was how itchy sanded fiberglass dust was. We painted the boat with a blue interior, white exterior and red copper bottom paint. Next project: get the 8-foot-long dinghy, nearly 4 feet wide out of the workshop, up the cellar stairs and outside. Dad removed (and later replaced) a partition wall between his workshop and access to the stairs. A lot of grunting, twisting and colorful language got our new sailing dinghy out of the basement, onto Dad's truck, then onto the pound boat and over to the island for its introduction to the water.

While this pram introduced us to sailing, it did not sail very well. As my older brothers gravitated to larger faster outboards, the dinghy was left to me. I recall a few times when we towed it behind my dad's boat, and water would shoot up the centerboard trunk and fill it with water. As I found myself rowing as much, or more than sailing, I decided to convert it to fit an outboard motor.

The sailing dinghy in 2009 under the beach house.

SETTING LEADERS

With earnings from digging clams, trapping, spearing and cleaning eels, and other odd jobs, I finally got enough money together to buy my first outboard motor, a 3 horsepower Evinrude! I remember the day that my dad bought it for me at the dealer in Islip. Late in the afternoon, as the pound boat passed the beach house on its return trip from Islip, my dad held the outboard up high over his head with one hand to show me he had it! I was so excited! I ran down the dock to meet the boat and see my first outboard motor!

This is a 3 horsepower Evinrude like my first motor.

And so began my education on marine engines. This being a 2-stroke engine, it was necessary to mix oil with the gas for proper lubrication. The integral tank on this motor held a little less than ¾ of a gallon. I carried with me a red steel-domed gas can that held 2½ gallons for reserve. The recommended oil/gas mixing ratio was ½ pint of oil to 1 gallon of gas—that's a one to sixteen ratio. By today's standards, that is a very oil rich mixture, considering many current outboards use a ratio of up to one to a hundred. Let's say I became quite proficient at cleaning fouled spark plugs. And with math not being my strength and a scarcity of graduated measuring containers on the island, this oil/gas ratio became a sort of estimation exercise.

On the dock, the Sunrise Fish Company had two 55-gallon drums held on their sides in heavy wooden cradles. One drum was diesel; used in the pound boat and scow for fuel and also used for thinning the copper paint and for cleaning tools and hands. The other drum was gasoline; used in the skiff, the Hyster sharpies and various outboard motors. Each drum had a steel spigot about 18 inches off the dock so a container could be filled beneath it. There was a clipboard on the wall inside the second net shed where you were *supposed to* mark down your name and how many gallons of gas you took so you could pay for it by the end of the summer. A little 3 horse outboard certainly didn't use that much gas … especially when you didn't always remember to mark it down on the clipboard.

Okay, the outboard was small, but so was the dinghy—and I wasn't too big either. I rigged a 3-foot-long aluminum pole to fit over the tiller arm of the motor so that I could steer from further forward in the boat for better trim. I would pull the cord to start the motor, insert the pole over the tiller, then slide the throttle lever all the way to full power. By leaning my weight way forward in the boat, I could just get the dinghy up on plane and achieve its fastest boat speed. Also, up on plane, it could scoot across really shallow water. As the water depth dropped below 8 or 10 inches, the engine skeg was just above the bottom, but the hull would "feel" the shallow water and actually lift a bit, increasing speed and reducing draft. I could really fly over those shoals … until I hit something … or the bottom.

Then I learned about shear pins. The propeller slides onto the shaft and the power is transmitted through a thin frangible steel rod called a shear pin. This pin runs through a hole in the shaft and sets into a slot in the propeller. It is intended to be like an electrical fuse protecting circuits whereby, in the event of striking an object, the shear pin would literally shear or break, protecting the rest of the power train. So, I always carried a small tool kit with spare shear pins, cotter pins and spark plugs, along with pliers, a screwdriver, a sparkplug wrench and a knife.

When a shear pin breaks, it is then in three pieces: one long piece that fits in the propeller slot and two smaller pieces from each end. My brother Bob showed me the trick of re-using these pieces if you didn't have a spare; first insert the long piece, then the two shorter bits. By inserting them this way, the broken parts are inside the prop slot and the solid parts bridge the gap between the shaft on the prop.

With this tiny little boat I ventured miles away; all the way down to Oak Island to visit friends. I got to know the labyrinth of channels through the meadows thoroughly—and where to find clams, crabs, eels and turtles. I would spend hours every day on adventures in my boat. (In later years, with a bigger faster boat, when the Coast Guard decided to pursue me for running at night with no navigation lights, I would make a quick dash through the meandering, shallow meadow channels, ducking behind a stand of tall reeds, which shielded my boat from their probing, powerful spotlight.)

Garveys

My oldest brother, Richard, was given a hand-me-down boat from our older cousin Nicky. This was a cross-planked (i.e., leaky) flat bottomed garvey with a covered-over aft deck and an outboard fitted in a well. With this arrangement, the motor was not clamped to the transom but was in a special "well," or hole, whereby the propeller shaft projected through the bottom a couple of feet forward of the stern. This allowed it to travel in shallower water, plus the aft deck could be used for crabbing or holding a seine net. He had a 5½ horsepower Evinrude that moved the boat pretty well. The most notable feature of this boat was that it leaked … badly. That's why he named it *Osmo* (osmosis).

Now Bob needed a boat. My dad set up a framing jig in the garage to build Bob a garvey. These were popular flat bottom boats that were well suited for the shallow waters around the island. They were relatively simple to build and used common materials like plywood reinforced with sawn oak frames. The boat had the typical squared off bow which Dad designed to have a bit of flare and shear to prevent hard slamming into waves. The overall length was about 12 feet with a 4-foot beam. Dad used Everdur bronze screws and copper rivets, combined with epoxy glue to assemble this boat of his own design. The copper rivets were a time-honored boat fastening method which provided a strong bond that would not loosen with pounding and vibration. Installing the rivets was a two-man job. First a slightly undersized hole was drilled for the copper nail through the oak frame into the plywood. A copper washer was placed over the nail, enlarging the head surface area, and the nail was hammered through the hole to the inside of the boat. On the outside, a copper washer was placed over the nail and then cut off with big diagonal cutters, leaving about an eighth of an inch stub. Then, the person on the outside held a heavy hammer or lead weight against the nail head, while the person on the inside used a ball peen hammer to flatten the copper nail stub, tightening and securing it against the washer and the frame. The more it was pounded on and peened over, the tighter the rivet pulled. As the boat was built upside down, the inside person had to work sitting on the floor under the boat.

For additional strength and to keep the water out, the entire bottom was covered with fiberglass cloth and coated with polyester resin. Since this was done in the open garage, the styrene smell was not as much of an issue as it had been when the pram was built in the basement. The completed boat was painted, turned right side up for some finishing touches on seats, floor gratings and paint, and was then ready to be lifted onto Dad's truck.

A typical Great South Bay garvey.

It wasn't long before I outgrew my little 8-foot pram and wanted a garvey too. Dad obliged by building yet another boat. He liked the look and admired the inherent strength of a slightly curved transom as seen in the new fiberglass Boston Whalers, combined with a bit of rounding up at the aft corners of the bottom. So, to build the transom, he laminated layers of plywood, weighted down with cement blocks between supports to provide the desired curve while the epoxy glue cured. Unlike Bob's boat with the flared bow (which I think made it a bit squirrely in following seas), my boat had a flat bottom from the squared off bow back to a couple of feet from the stern where the corners slightly rounded up to the transom. While this had a nice look to it, it made the boat tend to squat rather than providing beneficial lift when getting up on a plane.

For some reason, perhaps the extra cost of fiberglass and resin, Dad only fiberglass-taped the chines on this boat—and must have run out of resin, as the cloth was not wetted out and was porous. I recall my horror at seeing water seeping into the perfectly dry bottom after the initial launch in the Islip creek. Later, heavier coats of paint sealed it up—but it was disappointing. I fitted the boat with an 18 horse Evinrude which made the boat fly! This was a huge upgrade from my little pram, which was relegated to my younger sisters, Robin and Heidi.

This new fast garvey opened up my realm of travels—allowing me to zoom through the meadows, and taking me to new ventures, friends and parties on Fire Island. I even used it to commute across the bay to the waterfront campus of Dowling College in Oakdale when I was taking a summer course there.

Dad's Boats

We had other boats in the family. Before the pram and the garveys, when we just had the sharpie rowboat, my dad's boat was the *Skippy*. This was a lapstreak inboard, about 20 feet long. It had a big open cockpit and a cabin up forward. Dad always complained about it being a "wet" boat; that is … something about the flare to the bow would shoot spray back over the helm and cockpit. I recall a family cruise down to Zack's Bay where we spent a few nights … in the rain. This boat wasn't really set up for cruising. I imagine it was a real challenge for my parents with three little boys aboard!

Mom, Richard and Bob in the Skippy, *1947.*

Skippy

The *Skippy* was driven by a 6-cylinder gasoline engine housed in an engine box in the center of the cockpit. Sometime in the late 1950s or early 1960s, Dad sold the *Skippy* and bought a brand new 18-foot Thompson. This was a beautifully built lapstreak boat with abundant varnished mahogany. It was powered by a huge 30 horsepower Evinrude set in a well-type transom so waves could not swamp over the stern.

This is similar to the 18-foot Thompson.

We had many years of family fun, as well as innumerable trips back and forth across the bay and to Captree in this boat. The fancy varnish was a bit fussy for a fisherman's boat and most of it was later painted over. With water intrusion around the windshield and other dry rot areas, Dad decided to remove the windshield and most of the forward deck, and relocated the helm amidships for an early version of what is now called a center console boat. There was a parade of engines on the back. Dad half-jokingly used to say that *'the best thing about outboard motors is that you could simply unscrew the mounting clamps and dump them overboard!'* After the anemic 30 horsepower Evinrude, despite being a loyal Evinrude/Johnson fan, he tried a 45 horsepower Mercury. It seemed there were lots of issues with the Merc, so that didn't stay around long. And so, it was followed by a huge 75 horsepower Evinrude!

For a few summers, Bob and I worked in Sunrise Fish Company's retail fish store in Islip. Living on the island, we had to get up early, have a quick breakfast and commute five miles across the bay to the mainland with Dad's boat. We did this in all weather: storms, wind, rain and fog. I recall one foggy morning with visibility only a few hundred feet. We followed our usual compass course, then came upon an unfamiliar landfall—which turned out to be East Islip—several miles to the east of our destination. Looking again at the compass, I saw an errant screwdriver had been left by the compass, skewing it and our course. Recognizing this, we followed the shoreline back to the west until familiar landmarks came into view. Of course, this made us a bit late for work and we had to listen to old Harry Slonick, the ultimate vision of W.C. Fields in every way, saying, "… so where was ya's ancha'ed dis mornin'?" (Harry was well known for his clam chowder, which we helped make in 20-gallon pots; *'you start with a bushel of clams.'* He would also disappear with the remark, "I gotta go check the chowda" … and he'd be back in 30 minutes with a beery smile and a glowing alcohol-red nose.)

Dad had devised an ingenious mooring for this boat. Typically, docking the boat required a U-turn to bring the portside up against an automobile tire fender secured to a piling. A short "nipper line" was secured to the tire line while the bow and stern lines were made fast. After the boat was unloaded, a long line was removed from a piling and secured to the bow cleat. This line led to a block on the end of the jetty. The line then led to another block closer in on the jetty and then back to the end of the dock where the boat was secured. To operate this system, the bow line to the dock was eased, the nipper line was released and then the stern line was eased. The pulley system line was hauled on, pulling the boat away from the dock until the stern line tightened. This held the boat out so that strong winds and big waves would not push it up against the dock or pilings.

BEETLE CAT

One would expect that, after spending the entire day on the pound boat fishing in the ocean, then bringing the boat to Islip to pack out the fish followed by another trip across the bay in the late afternoon to bring the boat back to the island, the last thing my dad would want to do is spend more time on a boat. But he had always wanted a Beetle Cat sailboat—so he bought one for the family. After a long day of fishing, he enjoyed taking the Beetle Cat out for an evening sail.

Setting Leaders

The Beetle Cat design had been around since 1921. This beamy, 12-foot-long gaff rigged boat had a wide cockpit, separated by a centerboard trunk and a big sturdy tiller to control the barn-door rudder. It was a comfortable boat to sail alone or with a gang of kids aboard. Late afternoons on the south shore of Long Island guaranteed brisk southwesterly breezes, providing spirited sailing conditions. Dad constructed more than one replacement oak tiller after it snapped when a jubilant sailor failed to reef in time. The shoal draft made it a pleasure to ghost along silently through the shallow green meadows, quietly approaching great blue herons intent on catching fish.

Beetle Cat

We enjoyed the Beetle Cat for a good number of summers. But alas, being a wooden boat, it needed more care than simply pulling it up in the reeds at summer's end. Had we brought it home to the mainland for the winter, it would have likely received more love—but it seems there are always other priorities, and when we finally returned to the Beetle Cat, it was too late. The elements had not been kind. Too much rain water had collected in her bilges. Too much rot riddled her hull to realistically bring her back to life.

Beach Kid Creations

Though barely considered "boats," we played around in anything that floated ... or nearly floated. Back then the Coast Guard station on Fire Island had a dump next to their property where some interesting things could often be found. One was an apparently condemned, grey canvas covered, balsa wood life raft. It measured about 4 by 6 feet and was a foot thick. We nailed a few boards on it to make a deck and it was great fun to swim from.

The beach kids enjoying the Coast Guard dump life raft with the Skippy *and the scow in the background.*

"Hey Ron," asked Richard, just home for summer break from college, "can I try your skateboard?" In less than 5 minutes we were off to the emergency room with a broken arm. Commercial fishermen needed two strong arms. Richard's plan for summer earnings working with Dad on the pound boat fell apart.

Not easily deterred, Richard encased his arm cast in a plastic bag and set off for the flats with the battered 10-foot Styrofoam hull of what used to be a Snark sailboat. On this "boat," with his cast protected in plastic, he treaded for clams, picking them up with his other hand. Clams live in sand and mud. When they are dug up, they carry this mud with them onto the boat. Richard did very well digging clams and was able to earn some money despite his disability. His cast had to be replaced several times because it became so incredibly dirty, rank and stinky from sand, mud and clam juice. Unlike his garvey, the Styrofoam boat never leaked or had to be bailed.

Bob and I took a drifted-up pallet, nailed a few planks on the open end, then filled it with corked and sealed glass bottles that we found along the shore for flotation. Most of these were empty liquor bottles. For some reason fishermen were great sources of empty liquor bottles! We then closed up the end of the pallet and the *SS Bottlecraft* was launched! It actually supported us pretty well, if you didn't mind all the clunking and clinking of bottles.

Having a great fascination with sunken wrecks, and knowing that they attracted fish and other sea life, we decided to make one. There was an old, beyond redemption, 12-foot wooden dory that had weeds growing through it for years. We dragged it down to the water and, being made of wood, it floated … sort of. Rummaging around various junk piles, we gathered a collection of rusty pipes, plumbing fittings, concrete chunks and anything else that we could find to ballast the boat to the bottom. And we knew just the spot to sink this boat. Back in the meadows at a sharp turn in a creek, the current had scoured the water depth down to about 8 feet. Here it would be away from any boat traffic and it was deep enough to make it interesting. We bailed the boat out for easier towing. The ballast would be put aboard at the sinking site so that it wouldn't go down before we got there.

After a slow 20-minute tow with a garvey, we put on our masks, snorkels and flippers to assess the best bottom location for the boat. While the dory was slowly filling with water on its own, we started to add the heavy ballast. With 3 kids aboard, the water level rose higher, covering the seats, then finally washing over the gunwales. As it sank below the surface, we swam down with it and watched it settle on the bottom with a cloud of sand and mud. We dove all around it and had a great feeling of satisfaction. In fact, that wreck was there for many years. It collected a forest of sea growth and was home to a lot of little fish. Once we brought one of Mom's big galvanized wash tubs to the wreck. We secured lines on the handles and tied it to the wreck. Then, with a hand bilge pump and a long hose, we pumped air down into the inverted tub. We could then dive down from the surface and come up under the tub where we could breathe inside the air pocket.

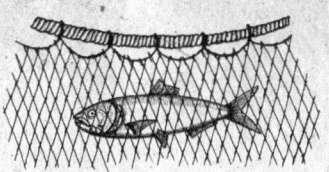

The Beach Houses and Net Sheds

The "first" net shed, was "first" because it was situated furthest out on the dock. It was the first net shed that you came to when you walked off the boats. It was typical "shed" built, i.e., it was a rectangle, roughly 12 feet wide, maybe 18 feet long with 8 feet of headroom. The roof was higher in the front and sloped back, away from the large sliding door. The heavy wooden door was hung on top with wheel-like rollers that ran in a steel track. It took a lot of leaning into for a small kid to shove it open.

Inside was the heady aroma of old copper paint, musty nets and ropes, sweat and the sea. Heaped inside the door, was a spare "pocket"—the netting with the smallest mesh—where all the fish were channeled before hauling them aboard the boat. The sides of the shed held the "hearts" and "apron" sections of the net system. They were made from larger mesh and functioned to direct fish to the "funnel," which led them into the pocket. These were a bit lighter in weight and so were folded or flaked back and forth in rectangular piles at each end of the shed.

All of these nets had been in service before. When they were taken in from the ocean, they were hoisted by the winch on the scow and lifted some 60 feet off the deck, creating a cascade of seawater, seaweed, and sometimes even live seahorses! As kids, we would run under the dripping net to pick the seahorses off of the deck. They would wrap their little tails around our fingers as we placed them in a cedar bucket of seawater. We often kept them in large glass jars that we prepared with sand in the bottom and live seaweed for them to cling to or hide in. To aerate the water, we periodically put a drinking straw in the water and blew bubbles in the tank—more than once mistakenly sucking in some salt water. We also witnessed male seahorses giving birth to hundreds of baby seahorses! Yes, it is the male that carries the fertilized eggs and hatches them out.

The heavy, dirty nets were heaped up on the decks of the scow, noticeably settling the boat deeper in the water. On the way back towards the inlet, some waves would wash over the bluff bows of the scow and run down the deck—exciting stuff for kids—maybe not so much for my dad and uncle who kept the bilge pumps running on this old wooden work boat.

When secured to the dock at the island, the nets would be systematically hoisted up with the scow's tall booms and pressure washed with a fire hose to remove sea growth, sea roses, weed and algae. There were times that the washed off sea roses would pile nearly knee deep on the scow deck and docks. When the net washing was done, the hose was used to blast the dock and decks clean. Sometimes, when there was too much buildup of sea roses, the crew would take the scow well out into the bay to wash the decks off. Being live creatures, when sea roses were drying out, they gave off an awful stink. After a day or two of dry breezy weather with the net suspended from the scow boom, any leftover sea roses would dry out to a crispy, brittle, shredded wheat-like consistency. Then the crew would use 2-foot-long flat pieces of wood, worn smooth from years of use, to swat the remaining dried sea roses off of the net. The brittle sea roses crumbled to dust which blew with the wind and fell through the cracks in the dock, piling inches deep underneath.

Every square inch of the nets and the supporting lines were inspected and repaired as needed. One of the kid jobs was to re-load the netting needles with twine. The netting twine came in large skeins, like a looped coil, that was placed on a cone shaped wooden spool, and was suspended from the ceiling in the big net shed. As the end of the white nylon twine was pulled, the spool slowly turned to feed out the required amount of twine which was carefully loaded back and forth on the plastic netting needle. The freshly loaded needle was then given to a crewman who used it to deftly secure an end with a becket or square knot on the net mesh next to a hole. The needle passed through adjacent net meshes and the hole soon disappeared as new meshes were woven. In the hands of an experienced fisherman, this repair happened in a blur of rapidly moving hands—until his razor sharp, wooden handled pocket knife was whipped out to cut off the end of the twine. Then on to the next one …

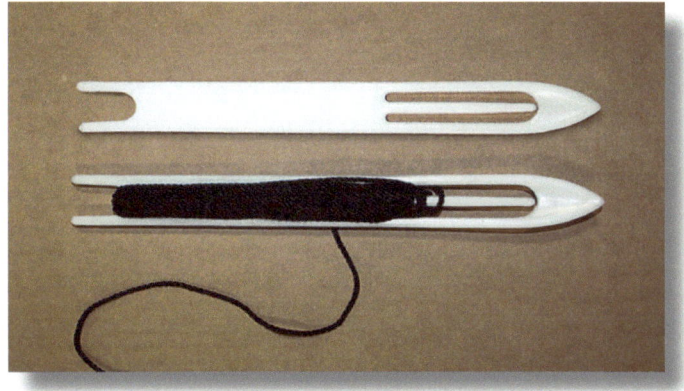

Netting needles.

Every fisherman carried a pocket knife. The favored one was made by a company called Case Knife. It was a simple single 3-inch blade knife folded into a brass riveted wooden handle. My dad and his brothers all had the same style knife, so they each carved a Roman numeral in the handle corresponding to who was first born, second and so on. My dad, being brother number 4, always had IV on his knife. These knives were in daily use and were kept razor sharp through repeated treatments on whetstones. In time, the blades were honed down to a narrow sliver of steel.

When there were large holes or tears in a net, the crew sewed in prepared netting panels which was more time efficient than weaving one net square at a time.

In earlier days, the nets were made of cotton twine. Cotton nets would only last for a few years before they weakened or rotted and had to be replaced. When modern nylon twine netting was available, the extra cost was well worth the added strength and longevity. The old cotton netting was relegated to placement between the pilings to help support the jetty.

After the nets dried and repairs had been made, they were carefully rolled up, or folded, depending on which sections they were, and then were loaded onto a large heavy-duty wagon which was pulled and pushed to the first net shed for storage. When it came time for them to go into service, replacing the nets in the ocean that needed to be cleaned, they would again be brought out on the wagon and preparations would be made to "tar" them.

These nets weren't actually "tarred" in the black sticky sense. That was just the name used for the process of coating the nets with copper paint to retard sea growth. Without this protection, the nets would be covered with sea roses, various sea weeds, mussels and barnacles within weeks. The weight of the heavy growth could break lines and poles and make it difficult to operate the traps.

The copper paint was purchased in heavy 55-gallon drums in an extremely concentrated solution containing a very high copper content. At the end of the dock was the tar rack which was situated above the tar pit. The tar pit was a wooden tank, measuring 8 feet long, 6 feet wide and 5 feet deep. The lip or edge of this tank extended about 14 inches above the surrounding dock. It was enclosed with a heavy canvas-sheathed wooden cover. To prepare the solution, a drum of copper paint was rolled over to the edge of the pit. The end bungs were unscrewed and the drum was tipped to rest on the edge of the pit while the viscous, rich red colored, concentrated copper paint oozed out. While this was draining, a drum of diesel fuel was also tipped and poured into the pit.

A pair of sturdy oak oars, thickly coated with dried copper paint from years of use, was used to scrape the bottom of the pit and mix and thin the copper paint to the right consistency for dipping the nets. After the copper paint drum was emptied, it was refilled several times with diesel oil, rolled and swished around to dissolve and capture all of the expensive paint. Experience had taught the men how full to make the pit to prevent overflowing when the nets were lowered in.

Right next to the tar pit was the tar rack. This was an elevated sloped platform, about 9 feet wide and 14 feet long with its upper end 7 feet above the dock. The rack had 2 by 4s spaced about 3 inches apart and 16-inch-high side boards. Below the slats was canvas-covered wood that channeled down into the pit. The net would be strapped—a spliced loop of rope was wrapped around the net and looped through itself as an attachment point for the lifting hook from the scow boom. The net would then be lifted up and lowered into the copper paint in the tar pit. Sometimes boot-clad workers would step on top of the net to weigh it down under the copper paint. The stirring oars were also used to push the net down for a good soaking. After it was completely saturated, the winch was used to slowly lift the net, streaming with copper paint, and the crew carefully spread it onto the tar rack. Excess copper paint gushed through the slats and flowed in rivulets back into the tar pit. The air was filled with the tangy metallic aroma of copper paint and diesel. The cover was dragged back onto the pit leaving about a foot open to accept the draining paint.

Mom, Heidi and Robin next to the tar rack.

Setting Leaders

Depending on weather conditions and the forecast, the crew might cover the heaped drying net with copper-stained canvas tarps. After a day or two, the pit was covered and the net was hoisted up onto a wagon and spread out on the dock to finish drying. Usually, the pocket section of the net was hoisted to the full extent of the boom (called two blocks) and left to air dry like a big tent.

The apron and heart sections of the net were strung out in parallel lines down the length of the long dock. These sections were designed to merely hang in the water, nearly to the bottom, to channel the fish into the pocket. Like all of these nets, they were supported by large poles on the top. Heavy link chain was used to weigh the lower ends down. With each link about 7 inches in length, the chains were strung out alongside these sections of net on the dock. The job of tying this chain to the nets often fell to my brothers and me. The line used was referred to as six-thread. This was an aromatic quarter inch diameter manila line with small sharp fibers sticking out of it and a natural oily feel. Unless you had built up calluses from handling lines for several weeks, your hands would become red and sore after spending a few hours working with it. New six-thread was supposed to have a breaking strength of 620 pounds. Maybe because it was cheap—maybe because they seemed to use miles of it—my dad used six-thread for almost everything.

The aprons are spread out on the dock. The chain has been tied on. At the end of the dock, the newly copper-painted pocket is hoisted up by the scow's forward boom for drying.

Back to tying on the chain—picture this: it is a beautiful summer day—you are at the beach, or at least on an island in the bay—surrounded by boats going by, gulls calling, the lighthouse picturesque across the water—maybe your friends go by in their boats to go skiing, or clamming and fishing … or are just heading to the beach. You are sitting on a copper paint-stained wooden dock with two rows of several hundred yards of heavy chain stretched out next to one-inch manila lines on the lower edges of the nets, all dripping sticky with wet copper paint. You must tie rolling hitches securing the chain links to this line. The line goes through the chain link, around the line three times to form a locking hitch, then a back hitch, then with the ever-present pocket knife, you cut the six-thread and go on to the next one. Copper paint covers your hands, your arms, your legs—scratch your face? Now it's on your face too!

Finally, you get in a rhythm and it seems like you might just be able to finish most of this today—then you drop your pocket knife through the cracks between the planks in the dock! You can squint and see it down there 16 inches below—but it is at least 25 feet from the edge of the dock and there is no room to crawl under there past the support beams. Off to the machine shop where Dad had years ago crafted a coat hanger type affair with a flexible copper wire noose on the end. Just insert the grabber through the open slat between the dock boards and work the open loop around the knife handle—pull it tight and carefully pull it up. Now, back to work.

Lastly, clean up starts with washing your hands in a filthy, rusty 5-gallon pail of diesel fuel. More diesel on a rag helps clean your face and legs. Then it's time for a swim … leaving an oil slick.

Setting Leaders

The first net shed. Note the single bare light bulb at the corner of the roof and the brass water spigot.

The first net shed had two very unusual characteristics for a building on a small isolated island: one was that it sported a large unshaded bare light bulb and secondly, it had a brass water spigot.

The light bulb was mounted high up on the southwest corner of the building where, on the rare instances that it was used, it cast a bright glaring halo of light around a wide perimeter of the dock.

There were times in the late 1950s when there was a run of small tuna. Early in the day, after the fish traps were raised, the men would fillet the tuna on the boat on their way back in from the ocean. When they reached the dock, the tuna fillets were salted down and soaked in brine in wooden tubs. The tubs were placed in the net shed out of the sun, iced down, and heavy canvas covers were put over them for insulation. The fish soaked in the brine all day which removed the blood and made the flesh lighter and not as strong tasting. Then in the evening, the men, their wives and children gathered under the light to process the fish for canning. Planks were spread on upended 55-gallon oil drums to form work tables. The tubs of soaking tuna fillets were brought out from the shed and were rinsed in wooden buckets of seawater, then passed on to the women who trimmed and stuffed the fish in clean Ball jars. Each glass lid was fitted with a new red rubber gasket and placed lightly on the jar without sealing the wire locking assembly. The filled jars were stacked in large boiler pots which were then lugged down to the fishermen's houses and put on top of the kerosene-fired stoves. These large blue-speckled enameled boiler pots were stacked full of the glass Ball jars and the pot was filled with 4 inches of water. Typically, the fishermen would then go to bed as they had to rise very early in the morning to go fishing again. The wives had the duty of tending to the boiling pots for 3 or 4 hours into the night (though they too got up early to make the fishermen their breakfast at 6 a.m.). Following the boiling operation, the wire clamps sealing the glass lids on the jars were secured and the jars were inverted while they cooled. This process ensured that the gasket did not leak and that all air was expelled from the jars. The cooling jars contracted, forming a vacuum to preserve the tuna.

The entire process; the swishing of buckets of seawater being drawn off the end of the dock, the fishermen's glowing cigarettes, the blur of activity in the fish preparation, the shouts of playing children—all under the glow of the first net shed light—presented a Norman Rockwell painting in my memory … not to mention numerous winter dinners of tuna casserole.

The electricity powering this light came from nearly the other end of the small island. In those days, there was a generator house near our beach house. It was a typical shed-style roof covering a ten by twelve-foot square building. There were two gasoline powered generators which provided 32-volt direct current to a large battery bank. The air inside this shed had a unique aroma of lube oil, gasoline, and battery off-gassing. A pair of heavy wires led from an electrical control box to the 9 or 10 houses and sheds of the fish camp. All the lights and equipment were 32-volt dc.

On wash days, my mom would fire up one of the generators to operate her old classic GE wringer washer which was set up with a 32-volt dc motor. My dad had instructed my mom on how to run the generators, and had insisted that the most important thing was to check the engine oil before starting the air-cooled engine. Well, one time Mom started the generator and got busy washing the clothes when she remembered that she hadn't checked the oil! She hurried into the generator house and unscrewed the oil dipstick … while the engine was running! Oil spurted out in a geyser, spraying all over her face, hair, arms and clothes. Oil covered everything in the room. Fortunately, the engine had not been running long so it wasn't too hot—but what a mess! This has been a favorite story in the lore of my family for years.

In later years, this dc generator/battery set up was "modernized" with a Kohler liquid cooled, 4-cylinder 115-volt alternating current generator that was carbureted to operate on bottled propane gas. Then all the equipment and appliances used at home on the mainland could be used at the beach! This machine had a circuit that would automatically start the generator if a light switch or other appliance called for power. After stored nets and gear were moved over, the new generator was installed in the second net shed. Tucked in the southwest corner, the exhaust pipe exited through a copper-lined hole in the wall, then made a 90-degree downward bend to mate with a large muffler, which exhausted a foot above the sand, where a small crater was created by the gases.

Above the engine was a panel of analog gauges showing coolant temperature, oil pressure, voltage and amperage. To the right of the generator were two large 100-pound propane cylinders which fed through a manifold and then through copper tubing to the special propane carburetor on the side of the engine. With this new ac generator, new wires were run to various houses and sheds. All of the lights and appliances had to be changed to accommodate the new power system.

Back to the other unique item on the first net shed; the brass water spigot. On a small isolated island surrounded by salt water, where did the fresh water come from that fed that spigot? As fresh water is less dense than salt water, it tends to "float" on top of salt water. Watching a rain storm pelt down upon the surface of the sea, it can be seen that the fresh water rain droplets tend to hover on the surface for a moment before dissolving. On this sandy island, rain water filters down through the sand until it meets the salt water a few feet below the surface. Since it is lighter than the salty water below, it lays like a lens below the sand. A well point, which is a special type of perforated pipe, was driven a few feet down through the sand. Suction piping was led back to a pump and fresh water was drawn up from the ground.

The water pump shared space in the old generator shed. Located over 100 yards from the well point, the water pump was a positive displacement type device which had a 4-inch diameter brass piston in a cast iron housing. The piston was activated by heavy gears in an oil bath, driven by an 18-inch diameter cast iron pulley belted to an electric motor. The water was sucked in by the piston and pushed under pressure into a 4-foot diameter by 7-foot-tall galvanized water tank. Near the top of the tank was a pressure gauge indicating the pressure of the air column above the water. Typically, the pressure would reach 35 psi before switching off the motor. The operating water pump made a wonderful cacophony of sounds; it started with a subtle "click," which was the pressure switch telling the motor to turn on. There would be about a 10 to 15 second delay while the generator automatically turned on. Then the electric motor whirred to life with the flap of the V-belt on the pump pulley, the gushing squeak of the piston, the splashing sound of the oil-bathed gears and a gentle clunk as water was pushed into the tank under pressure. The water pipes led from there to all the houses and way, way down to the end of the dock to the first net shed spigot. The original pipes were made of galvanized iron. They imparted rust to the water and were gradually replaced piece by piece with copper, and later with plastic piping.

When the old 32-volt generators were removed from the generator shed, it created added space for growing families. Soon it became a bunk house for my brother Bob and myself. While the generators were gone, we still shared the space with the water pump. So, if someone felt the call of nature at 3 a.m. and flushed their toilet … we would hear the gentle "click …" and knew to expect a 10-minute chorus from the water pump until it reached pressure.

While I always remember having running water and indoor plumbing on the island, many of the beach houses relied on outhouses for their needs. Some of these can still be seen behind the shacks.

The necessary depository for the bathroom waste was a simple, fairly shallow pit dug into the sand, usually surrounded by porous cement blocks to keep the sand from caving in. This cesspool was located about 10 feet from the house and was connected in the old days by ceramic or iron pipe—now PVC is used. Early in the spring was a good time to dig out any remaining waste and sand that had filled in to ensure enough capacity for the summer.

Visitors and guests on the island were often encouraged to conserve precious water supplies with little poems placed in the bathrooms, such as: *'In this land of sea and sun, we never flush for number one.'* Or, *'If it's yellow, let it mellow.'*

Constant erosion to the island has caused salt water intrusion to the thin layer of fresh water making it no longer usable. Now the homes rely on catching rainwater from gutters on the roof and saving it in large plastic cisterns. Just as on a boat, a 12-volt electric water pump is used to pressurize the homes' water systems. Electric power comes from banks of 12-volt batteries charged by solar panels. Most houses also have small gasoline generators for occasional temporary use.

In the 1960s, growing up on the beach, we were initially amazed when we could actually watch a black and white TV there. We only got a couple of channels, depending on how you turned the antennas, and the generator was only on for a couple of hours a night—but it was something new for the island. Now, with advances in charging systems, electronics, cell phones and the like, residents on the island, like my sister Robin, can set up a mobile office with computers connected to the internet, and have just about every other convenience found on the mainland.

That first net shed also contained something that was as intriguing and forbidding to young kids as it was dangerous—DYNAMITE! Yes, secured with chains high in the upper corners of the shed were heavy padlocked steel grey-painted boxes, red-stenciled "DANGER." These rarely moved boxes contained sticks of dynamite and electric blasting caps. You can just imagine the thoughts of havoc that ran through our mischievous and wildly imaginative young minds.

So, what did a small pound trap fishing operation need with dynamite? The ocean nets were supported by a myriad of long, large-diameter tree trunks called poles. Many of these poles were 14 to 16 inches in diameter at their base, tapering to 10 to 12 inches at the top, and 35 to 40 feet in length. Therefore, the offshore poles, standing in 60 feet of water, were spliced together to provide the needed length. To splice two poles together, they would be placed on the deck of the scow, overlapping each other by 10 or 12 feet. One inch nylon line was tied with multiple hitches and super tightened by leading the line to a power winch. Over the 10 to 12-foot splice area, at least four sets of hitches would be made. The result was a strong, stiff, but somewhat flexible pole, 95 feet in length. Safely lifting and handling this heavy long pole would be challenging even from a stable platform. But these poles were maneuvered by booms off the deck of a vessel rolling with the ocean swells.

An early spring supply of new "poles," the back side of the tar rack and the pound boat with the scow behind it.

    The operation to "set" or "pump" a pole so it would securely stand up to support the heavy nets and rigging in the turbulent ocean took skill, experience and a lot of hard work. The pole lay on deck with the base or bottom facing the bow of the scow. The crew used a 2-inch diameter by 20-foot-long galvanized steel pipe that had a threaded fitting on top to accommodate the attachment of a fire hose. The pipe was secured to the lower end of the pole where heavy nails had been pounded which were then bent over the pipe to cradle it in place. At the upper end of the pipe was a strong nylon line which led along the length of the pole, held in position by several six-thread lines. Lengths of 4-inch diameter fire hose were arranged on deck and one end was screwed to the top of the pipe. The other end was fed by the scow's powerful water pump. The pole was carefully lifted with two booms, timing the ocean swells and the roll of the scow. The exact position to place the pole had been measured against the blueprint chart (and my dad's and uncles' memory and experience) and located by marked lines from the adjacent poles of the trap. The bottom end of the pole was lowered over the bow as the top end was lifted upward and forward. Guide lines were used by the crew to position the pole as it finally reached the ocean floor. When it was deemed to be in the right spot, the pump was engaged, sending a torrent of seawater down through the fire hose. The gush of water at the bottom of the pole blasted the seafloor sand

Setting Leaders

aside as the heavy pole gradually sank into the bottom. The poles were usually set 15 to 16 feet deep into the ocean floor. When the twine which marked the right depth reached the water surface, the pump was shut down and the nylon line that was secured to the pipe was wrapped on a winch and pulled up. The hose was also pulled up and all the gear was stowed.

A long solitary pole like this in 60 feet of water had to be connected to other poles so that it didn't sway with the ocean swells. So next came the job of rigging the various stay lines from the new pole to work with the complex web of other poles and lines in the pound trap system. Tall poles such as this surrounded the "pocket" section of netting. Because they had to hold and also lift the weight of the net filled with fish, the pole was stabilized by an offshore, smaller pole to help take the load. Much like a sailboat's mast, the pole had great strength in compression, but must not bend out of column or it could break.

Smaller poles for dock building were set up the same way as in the ocean. Here the fire hose can be seen attached to the pipe which is nailed to the next pole to be pumped.

To rig the lines and multipart block and tackle arrangements, a man had to climb or be hoisted to the top of the pole, much like a telephone lineman, and tie them on. When I was in grade school, a friend whose father worked for the electric company boasted that his dad climbed telephone poles. "Yeah," I would say, "my dad climbs poles out in the ocean!"

So … what about the dynamite?

Sometimes, especially after storms, a pole was discovered to be broken, usually well under the surface. Not only did the pole have to be replaced to support that part of the fish trap system, but the broken pole had to be removed. That's where the dynamite comes in. In the old days, they used a lead line sweep to locate the broken pole stump. A messenger line was used to drag an explosive charge down around the stump to, hopefully, break it off at the bottom. Since they could not see what was happening on the ocean bottom, it involved a bit of guesswork.

As kids growing up on the island, we were all water rats. We were always in and around and under the water; swimming, snorkeling and spear fishing. When we were in our teens, my dad was also keen on diving and with the guidance of his friend, a professional scuba diver for the police department, we began to invest in equipment, and were soon scuba diving in the ocean. Often after working the nets Monday through Saturday, with our encouragement, my dad would take us out to the pound nets and we would scuba around the nets—and sometimes in the nets! It is quite a thrill to have a 600-pound tuna swim by an arm's length away!

A stick of dynamite is about an inch in diameter and about a foot long. It is wrapped in a waxy brown paper, not red like in the cartoons. Dynamite requires a charge to make it explode. An electric blasting cap was used to set the dynamite off. The blasting cap would be wrapped in the middle of 12 sticks of dynamite which were tightly tied together with six-thread, and had two wires leading out of the bundle. A long black wire was spliced to these connections so the charge could be set off remotely.

At the age of 16, with a scuba tank on my back and a weight belt secured at my waist, I swam 60 feet down carrying a bundle of 12 sticks of dynamite! Hey … how many 16-year-olds get to do this? Though the water visibility was only a few feet, I followed the drag line down to the broken pole. With several passes of six-thread line around the pole, I secured the dynamite bundle to its base, then followed the black wire back up to the boat.

Once I was back on board, the ends of the wire were led to a large 12-volt battery on the deck. First the black ground wire—then … tension building … touch the red wire to the positive terminal. A dull thud was felt through the deck—then a huge geyser of water and smoke erupted nearby! We went out in the sharpie with nets and scooped up dozens of stunned fish; black fish, bigauls, pilot fish, trigger fish.

Pretty exciting stuff for a kid. As an alternative to dynamite, we had actually tried to use a two-man lumberjack saw underwater to cut a stump off manually—but it was impossible to secure oneself to be able to push and pull the saw. Plus, the exertion used up the air in the scuba tank very rapidly.

The second net shed, as previously noted, became home to the Kohler generator. This shed primarily stored the heart and apron parts of the pound nets. The apron sections were folded in 5-foot-wide piles about 4 feet high along the east and north walls. The heart netting was in a big 9-foot diameter round ball in the center of the shed. Over the large sliding door was a wooden rack that held spare oars, boat hooks and gaffs, and other long slender gear like tangled bamboo snapper poles and crab nets.

The next net shed was the **big net shed**. This was town hall—the capitol—the center of operations—the meeting place—the Taj Mahal …

Okay, maybe that was a bit much. Not only was the big net shed the *biggest* net shed, it didn't even have a "shed" roof—it had a peaked roof of galvanized corrugated steel, painted black. But sloping to the east side was a shed-type roof. This provided an ample attic area for the storing of wondrous things—not to mention hiding places for kids' fantasies.

Heidi and Robin Schaper at a rehearsal for a puppet show and skit in the big net shed. They would invite everyone on the island, charge a small admission and serve lemonade.

The big net shed was big compared to the other sheds. It measured almost 30 feet across the south facing dock entrance and perhaps 25 feet deep to the north. The one big heavy sliding door took both hands of a kid on the steel handle, leaning heavily to the right to move it on its overhead tracks. Once open it presented a good 8-foot wide by 6½-foot high aperture. The threshold ramped up several inches with a carved wooden doorstep.

The floor inside was solid wooden planked, unlike the other net sheds whose floors were the dock boards with one-inch spaces in between them. Natural lighting was enhanced by windows in each wall, plus one in the sliding door. Except for the one in the door, the windows could open by sliding them sideways in a wooden track. The windows would lock by placing a nail loosely in a hole at the edge of the frame. Each shed door had a large galvanized steel hasp and brass padlock. The keys for the locks were hidden down by the sides of the shed, hanging on a nail or inserted in a crack in the wooden support structure. During the summer, when people were around all the time, none of the sheds were locked.

Entering the big net shed, on the immediate left, was a window that was always laced with spider webs and dead flies. In the corner was a 55-gallon drum standing on end with a hand crank pump on top. A U-shaped pipe could be swung to the side, a container put under the pump outlet, and by turning the crank, 30 weight lube oil could fill a container. This was the lube oil used for the various engines in the boats and on the island. The top of this oil drum always had a layer of residual oil on it (kids just loved to turn that pump handle … and it leaked onto the drum top). Behind the drum, there were 2-inch flat boards forming the rungs of a ladder leading up to the loft. There were always small oily footprints on the steps from treading on the oil drum to get to the ladder. The ceiling, or bottom of the loft floor, was about 7 feet off the floor. When we got older, bigger and bolder, we would jump up to grab the 2 by 4 floor support in one of the openings and with practiced gymnastic moves, spin our legs up and over the 2 by 4 and swing into the loft.

The big net shed held every assortment of supplies; coils of line, spools of netting twine, skeins of netting, shackles and chain. In the back left corner was a 4-foot square locker that had been built by my uncle Nick to store his hard hat diving suit. The locker was painted grey and it had a door with numerous ventilation holes drilled into it. It was also locked with a hasp and padlock. Inside the locker was a sturdy horizontal pole to hold the heavy canvas diving suit. On a shelf above it was the huge brass diving helmet. The helmet was about 14 inches in diameter and had several porthole-like round windows in it. The bottom of the helmet had a flange that screwed it together with the canvas suit. On the floor were two huge lead weighted boots. Though I never did see this diving rig used, my dad told me that the one time he tried it, the suit filled with water when he was on the bottom! It was always a cool thing to show my friends.

In later years, the dive suit was removed (I think my cousin has the helmet) and the locker was filled with our "modern" dive gear: scuba tanks, regulators, wetsuits, masks, snorkels, spear guns, etc. We envied my dad's first wetsuit. The waters in New York were not particularly warm, especially in the inlet and ocean where the best diving and spear fishing was. These early wetsuits were 100% neoprene, with no strengthening lamination the way current suits are made. To struggle into the suit, a copious amount of talcum powder had to be applied to arms and legs or the neoprene would stick to your body and not slide on. Often, while pulling it onto your legs your fingernails would tear holes in the material. The first time using a wetsuit is interesting: the initial plunge into the water sends freezing-cold water channeling through every arm, leg and head opening—it is a bit of a shock until the layer of water next to your skin warms up. Then, until the correct amount of lead weights are strapped on to counteract the buoyancy of the suit, you bob like a cork. (In later years, the BC, or buoyancy compensator, was invented to more easily achieve neutral buoyancy.)

In the center of the room, 4 feet from the back (north wall) was a kerosene heating stove. This rusty 3-foot square device stood 4 feet tall and had a steel stovepipe off the back leading through a metal collar in the back wall, connecting to a chimney outside up above the roof. This was used by the crew for heat both early and late in the season as they prepared or stowed the gear. Often in the summer months, the stovepipes were removed and the stove was shoved back against the wall for more room.

All around the northeast corner and along the east wall was a broad shelf holding coils of rope, netting and twine. The floor also was stacked with reels of netting and boxes of line. The beams above held cone shaped wooden reels on which skeins of twine were loaded. The top of the reels had swivels which allowed the twine to spool off as it was loaded onto a netting needle. Netting needles were flat plastic (originally wood) devices measuring about one-inch wide, 1/8 inch thick and 11 inches long. One end was rounded or pointed so it could easily pass through the net "holes." The other end was notched to retain the twine strung between the end and the center spline. The needle could hold about 15 feet of twine. It was often a kid helper's job to reload the netting needles.

The loft in the big net shed was a fun place for a kid. Coils of line, reels of netting and bundles of rope could be moved around to make a concealed fort. Sometimes the crewmen came in while we were quietly hidden away in the loft. While there were no big secrets discovered, it was fun to "spy" and eavesdrop on their conversations.

In our early teen years, we thought it was great fun to prank the crewmen with such things as "booby traps." A favorite was to take a curved 24-inch

Setting Leaders

section of automobile tire (which was on hand as fendering material for the sharpies), fill it with water and empty beer cans, then position it at an open floorboard of the loft right over the doorway entrance. A piece of twine was tied between the end of the tire and a nail in the sliding door. As skinny young kids we could squeeze out through a few inches of opened doorway, then close the door completely. While we hoped that the next person to open the door would be Ward or maybe Larry, it was not well received if uncle Arie or Dad opened the door! Pulling the door open tripped the twine which pulled the tire over and dumped its watery contents, beer cans and all right on the head! Not everyone had our sense of humor.

Another prank that Bob and I pulled was on a weekend day when my parents hosted a large church group at the island for a clambake and swimming. There were always a lot of young girls and kids not too used to our "beach ways." The popular swimming spot was in the sandy cove formed by the jetty and the moored scow. So, there were ten or twelve people both wading and swimming there, enjoying themselves. When Bob and I had been out fishing with our dad the day before, they caught a good-sized shark. While the carcass of the shark was properly dressed, iced and sent to market, we had carefully cut off the 14-inch-high dorsal fin. We then found a flat board about 12 inches wide by 2 feet long. We drove long nails up through the board into the bottom of the dorsal fin. When placed on the water, the board floated just even with the water surface. Well before the swimmers had entered the water, we had strung clear fishing line from the stern of the scow over to just around the corner of the jetty. When the swimmers were all happy and splashing and giggling in the water, we slowly pulled the fishing line towards the scow. Seeing a 14-inch dorsal fin slicing through the water right through the swimmers sent them screeching and charging out of the water … while we had ourselves a good laugh!

The peak of the big net shed's roof was the highest point around. We would often climb up on that steep, pitched, black-painted, corrugated steel surface to watch for the approaching pound boat. After spying the boat, we would scurry down the roof, with feet liberally coated with powdery black paint, sometimes daring to leap across to the next nearby roof. Back down on the dock, we ran past the beach houses singing "the pom boat … the pom boat …" to alert all to come greet the boat and see what fish was for dinner. Before the boat appeared around the corner of Captree Island, flocks of seagulls took to the air from the sand dunes, seeking fish scraps for lunch.

The pound boat ("pom" to the kids) would slow as it passed the jetty as the crew tended to the two sharpies towed behind. The boat glided alongside the scow, fendered by two big truck tires hanging from the scow's rigging. Greeting the boat were a band of bathing suit-clad kids, a few moms and several dogs. Often folks living on nearby islands would come over with their small boats to see about getting a fish for dinner.

I recall a time when Grandpa Gremli pulled his boat around the port bow of the pound boat just when my dad had fired up the bilge pump. They caught a lot of squid that day, which meant the bilge was loaded with slimy black ink. A good-sized gasoline engine powered the bilge pump which discharged through a long 2-inch diameter rubber hose. The hose could also draw ocean water and be used for a general wash down of the boat. The hose was stowed in its bilge pumping position through a loop up on the bow facing to the port side. Just as Grandpa Gremli passed the hose outlet, it spewed a gush of gallons of nasty, smelly, black squid ink bilge water right in his face!

Just east of the big net shed was the **machine shop.** This clapboard building was about 8 feet wide and 30 feet long. Its hinged front door was on the left side of the narrow side of the building and faced out onto the main dock. Stepping inside, you had to be careful in bare feet as there were often sharp bits on the oil-soaked floor. Spanning the length of the right wall was a massive wooden planked workbench, fitted with a couple of large iron vices. Next to the door were shelves stacked with glass jars, and coffee cans filled with nails, screws, bolts, nuts and washers, and some of the largest galvanized dock spikes I have ever seen.

Next to the shelves, in the corner at the end of the workbench was one of four windows which provided light to the room. Each window had its own collection of spider webs, dirt and buzzing flies.

The wall behind the workbench had a few shelves and various hand tools supported by numerous driven nails. There was quite a collection of hammers, many with missing nail-pulling claws, screw drivers, pliers, hand drills, braces and bits for boring holes, and hand saws. Many of these tools would be considered antique even 60 years ago—but they were all regularly used. My dad and uncles would insist that all tools must be returned to exactly where they were taken from! There was an oil can with a little thumb lever to squirt oil out of a copper tube applicator. A well-aimed squirt could take down a buzzing fly in the window!

This shop with its workbench was the place to go with anything that needed repairing. Many an outboard motor was clamped to a board in the vice with mechanical manipulations and curses administered. Balky carburetors and ignition systems from various small engines were worked on—and old carburetors which had tried the last bit of patience from the mechanic could be found in the sand outside the back door where they had been thrown in frustration!

My brothers and I used some of those big galvanized dock spikes to make harpoons. In the vice, we hacksawed the head off the spike. We took a hefty wooden pole, about 1½ inches in diameter and 5 feet long, then drilled a hole in the end of the pole a couple of inches deep. Next, we hammered the cut off end of the spike into the hole. The tip of the spike was filed into a sharp point. Then, we hitched six-thread lines like we had seen on the harpoons in Moby Dick. We were ready for big game! To practice, we zoomed our boat past the huge wooden sign off the end of the island and aimed for the "O" in the notice about the State Boat Channel clearances.

While the harpoons stuck into the soft wood of the sign, when we finally got to try them on a real target in the ocean—a huge Mola mola, or ocean sunfish—our harpoons harmlessly bounced off the tough hide of the sunfish as if it were a truck tire! The pound boat crew had a good laugh.

The workbench also had an unusual special vice-like apparatus for fixing or fitting the brass end pieces on fire hose. There was a hole in the wall across from this vice through which the end of a fire hose could be inserted so that it lined up straight to the vice. When not in use, a little block of wood swung over the hole. I also recall the nameplate "PIPER" on that back wall, salvaged from a crashed plane many years before.

Along with various rusty cans of paint, varnish, bottom paint, turpentine and old paint brushes, there was a brass Pyrene fire extinguisher on the wall. While I never saw one of these used, they appeared everywhere in those days. I have since learned that phosphene gas, a toxic poison, was created from the mixture of carbon tetrachloride and the flame. That is likely why they disappeared from use.

Brass Pyrene fire extinguisher.

On the wall opposite the workbench, there were long two-man log cutting saws, large steel pry bars, crow bars and sledge hammers—and more shelves holding various bits of hardware, bolts and nails. Stuffed up under the eaves were rolls of tar paper, galvanized wire mesh, window screening and stove pipes.

Ward's house was the next building after the machine shop. This bungalow dated back to the time before the bridge was built, when the crew lived at the beach all week long. Back in the day, Ward lived here in this one room building. It had a bed, a couple of dressers and a sink on one wall. In later years it was used for storage.

Down a long narrow boardwalk behind Ward's house was the **men's lavatory**. This shed-type building measured about 8 feet square, had a couple of toilet stalls and a shower in the corner.

The next building was another **bunkhouse** for the crew. In later years cousin Jeannie and Ritchie Westerlind expanded it and made it into a nice beach house for them and their growing family. Later, cousin David Schaper used it for a beach retreat.

Mom in front of Jeannie and Ritchie's house.

The last net shed was a simple 10 by 14-foot shed with no windows and a large sliding door. It was usually used to store the leaders. The only remarkable thing I recall about this building was the lore that a stash of silver had been buried beneath it!

Ward and Bob in front of the last net shed, 1967.

All of these buildings faced onto **the dock.** This main dock was huge as it was the work space for spreading out the nets and leaders. It was nearly the size of a football field and was constructed of 8 to 10-inch-wide by 8-foot-long boards, supported by heavy 4 by 10-inch timbers. Locust poles supported the timbers above the sand. The inshore side of the dock was about 18 inches above the sand; the offshore end of the dock terminated in about 5 feet of water. This offshore end was faced with large timbers and pilings for docking the scow. The dock had to be strong enough to support the weight of the nets, leaders, and chain, plus sometimes a small tractor and sturdy wagon. Most of the dock was stained red from the copper painted nets.

At the east end of the dock, just before the narrow boardwalk to the beach houses, there was a wooden rack which held a couple of 55-gallon drums on their sides. A spigot was screwed into the end of the drums so that kerosene containers for the refrigerators, stoves and lamps could be filled. At the time, there were six crew and their families with homes on the island.

Setting Leaders

Uncle Arie and Aunt Kate's house was the first one on the left. Right out front was a cold-water shower. It was often a race for swimmers at the end of the dock to get there first for the best sun-warmed water before it ran cold. There was also a little brass knurled knob by the shower handle that plumbers use to vent plumbing lines. We used it to shoot out a jet of water for a drink.

Kate and Arie's house had a lovely wide porch across the front, decorated with numerous fishing floats and buoys which had been found snagged in the nets. Inside was a living room, a tiny kitchen, two small bedrooms and a bathroom with a tub.

In later years, after Kate and Arie had moved to Florida, I used the house when my sons, Tristan and Trevor, were infants. Later, Russell and Mary Westerlind moved in and lived there full time—even through a winter. Eventually they too moved to Florida, and my sister Heidi, Tristan and Trevor, now adults, took it over. Soon after adding numerous improvements, including a costly new roof, super storm Sandy literally washed it away, leaving only the cast iron bathtub. Subsequent rebuilding is another story.

1943 Arie's house

After Kate and Arie's house was **the cook house**. In the days before the Captree Bridge, when the fishing crew stayed on the island all week, the fish company had a cook to prepare all of their meals. The only cook I remember was Jim, who had a huge lovable Newfoundland dog named Jumbo. My mom tells me of a young Japanese lady they had as cook for a while. She reportedly bathed naked in the bay every morning at sunrise!

With Uncle Arie on the left, the crew chows down in the cook house. On the left is an icebox. The door on the left went into a walk-in pantry, lined with shelves holding cans and dry goods. On the right is the doorway to the cook's bedroom and bathroom.

In later years, my grandma, Tina Schaper, mother of Nick, Arie, Bill, Allen and Louis, spent summers in the cook house. Many happy evenings were spent with Grandma Tina there … eating her fried chicken (her recipe: in a cast iron skillet, start with one pound of butter, add onions and chicken, cook till tender), fateballen (Dutch donuts), and playing rummy. (Tina would scold slow card players with "Moses! You play too slow!")

Setting Leaders

The next house east was usually referred to as **Dickie's shack**. This cube-shaped building, 8 feet square with a flat roof, supposedly drifted up on the beach after a storm. It was propped up on 4 by 6 supports and locust poles. It had just enough room for a bunk, a small dresser and a little sink on the wall. Grandma Tina stayed there until she moved to the cook house. I recall my brothers and I joining her there to tell ghost stories in the dark. Some stories were made up as we took turns adding to the tale and passing around objects we had brought in to enhance the effect: *'... the dead body washed up on the beach and had dried up scratchy hair ...'* and a wad of dried seaweed would be passed around in the dark; *'... worms crawled out of his mouth ...'* as we passed around cold spaghetti. We always called on Grandma to tell the "Johnny and the Golden Leg" story. *'Johnny ... I want my leg. Johnny ... I want my leg ... GOTCHA!!'*

Then it became Dickie's shack. Yes, we referred to these as "shacks." Defined by the dictionary as a small crude building, usually without a foundation ... I guess the description fits. As a kid, especially as a teenager, it was great to have your own little bunkhouse separate from your parents' house.

Robin climbing the crow's nest with Bobby & Ronny's shack shown on the left.

Just north of Dickie's shack, down an even narrower boardwalk, was the old generator house, later **Bobby and Ronny's shack**. As described earlier, it used to hold the old 32-volt generators and still had the fresh water pump and tank.

Mary and Lou's house, Mom and Dad's, was the next place to the east. "The Beach House." First of all, get the Nantucket/Hamptons/Malibu beach house image out of your head. Our beach house started its life as a one room construction site shed. My dad bought it cheap, disassembled it, and loaded it onto the pound boat for a trip across the Great South Bay to be re-assembled above the sand upon locust poles. Through the years, as our family grew, my ever-skilled dad added rooms and amenities. The house now has 2 bedrooms, a large kitchen with dining room table, a living room, a full bathroom and a wrap-around porch with a million-dollar view of the Fire Island Lighthouse.

The Beach House

What it lacked were "normal" utilities: no electricity, no water or sewer service, no cable tv or garbage service. We now use oil lamps, solar panels and generators, and brackish ground water for washing and flushing. In earlier years, we drank the fresh water that was pumped out of the sand. It had no filtration except from the well point screen and no chlorine or other treatments—and we survived. As noted earlier, salt water intrusion eventually made it no longer drinkable. Then potable water had to be carried over with food and other supplies. Now the houses harvest rain water from the roofs, collected in large plastic tank cubes, and 12-volt pumps circulate the water through the plumbing systems.

In later years, my sister Robin took over responsibility for the beach house—which, due to constant shore erosion, was storm damaged, and the whole house had to be jacked up and moved inland.

The last house towards the east end of the island was **Uncle Nick and Aunt Sue's house.** I don't remember too much about this house except that it had an upright piano that Aunt Sue would play—and I recall being there with her, Grandma Tina and cousins, singing some of their favorite hymns: "Look to the Lighthouse, God's Lighthouse of Love," "What a Friend We Have in Jesus," and "Amazing Grace." There was also a glass enclosed front porch overlooking the bay. This house was the first to suffer from severe beach erosion and it was eventually moved by barge over to Fire Island. Years later, the only evidence that it had been there were a few left-over locust pilings and the rusted galvanized water pipe that now extended out into the bay.

While **beach house appliances** evolved over the years, they were usually well behind the more modern devices on the mainland that enjoyed full time utility service.

Beach families first used old-fashioned iceboxes to keep their food cool. The pound boat would bring fresh blocks of ice several times a week. The ice was put in a compartment in the upper end of the icebox. The food items needing to be kept the coldest were placed nearest the ice. When fresh groceries came over on the boat, the meats would be consumed first as they had the shortest shelf life. As the ice melted, it ran down a tube through the bottom of the icebox. There a funnel directed the water through a hole drilled through the floor to drip under the house into the sand. My mom completely cleaned the icebox every week before loading the newest groceries, so mildew was never a problem.

The icebox was eventually replaced by a kerosene powered refrigerator, and finally a nice big Servel propane refrigerator. This type of refrigerator is quite different from the compressor driven units most of us are familiar with. These old units utilized what is called the absorption process. The refrigerant was ammonia, sealed in a labyrinth of pipes, coils and evaporators. The heat of a kerosene or propane flame boiled and propelled the ammonia into the separator, then the condenser, then to the evaporator where it would cool down the refrigerator box. It is a fairly complex process, but being a sealed system, there were few problems except for keeping the burner and flue cleaned. As these were only used for a few months each year and then turned off, rust on the piping in the salt air usually did them in after a decade or two. After sitting, there were times the unit wouldn't work, even if it hadn't leaked. Local lore had it that the ammonia could be redistributed through the system by turning the refrigerator upside down and letting it sit inverted for a few days. This often worked!

My mom recalls purchasing a 3-burner kerosene stove in 1943 for $19.00. It had a glass one-gallon container that inverted at the side of the stove. This kerosene jug had to be refilled daily from the 55-gallon drum down at the dock. I am told that this was my job at the tender age of 5 or 6 years old! This stove was lit with wooden matches held in a wall-mounted dispenser.

In the 1950s, an upgraded stove was installed at the family home on the mainland and our old propane stove was moved to the beach house. This stove had been purchased in 1939 by Grandpa Koch, Mom's father. It is an enormous, heavy nickel-plated cast iron Anderson stove with 4 burners, a large side griddle, an oven and a unique pull-out drawer for broiling. It also has a large built-in pot for soups. This venerable stove has been serving the best early fishermen's breakfasts and the freshest fish dinners for over 60 years—and is still in near perfect operation.

Mom with the 1939 Anderson stove. The griddle on the left produced thousands of blueberry pancakes and tons of bacon over the years.

In addition to longevity, the stove has several unique features like this integral soup cooker.

Before the bridge was built across the Great South Bay, linking the mainland with Captree, Mom would write a weekly grocery list which was sent ashore with the pound boat. Roulston's, the local grocery store (this was before supermarkets), filled the order and delivered it to the boat at the dock in Islip before 4 p.m. when the pound boat would depart for the island. Grandma Tina Schaper had a German friend with a large garden. Each week she would send over a couple of bushels of her fresh seasonal vegetables—at the price of $2.00 per bushel!

In the summer, Mom would order maybe one roast and some franks for the week—then we had fresh fish or eels the rest of the week, plus homemade clam chowder and deviled clams. Mom and Aunt Kate would often go clamming at low tide, and then make Aunt Sue's clam chowder recipe.

In 1954, the Captree Bridge was completed from the mainland to Captree Island. Our island was no longer as isolated as it had once been. The bridge changed many factors of life on the island. Captree Boat Basin was a short boat ride away. The family car (station wagon, of course), could be parked there for an easy 20-minute ride to the mainland. Mom was no longer bound by her weekly grocery list to be filled by others and could drive herself to the grocery store, still on a weekly basis. The challenge came when she returned to Captree with a car full of groceries. This, of course, was long before cell phones were even dreamed of—so Mom would walk to the far end of the Captree fishing pier, take out her little plastic whistle, hope the wind was from the right direction and that someone working on the nets on the dock would hear her as she tweeted away and waited for them to wave back. Then my dad, or one of the crew, or one of my brothers, or I would jump in the skiff and head across the State Boat Channel to pick up Mom and the many brown paper grocery sacks and cardboard boxes filled with groceries.

Over the years, my mom collected quite a few anecdotes from people who had watched her hail her ride from across the water. Some were thrilled and mentioned something about *'pioneering'* and *'like being out of the movies!'*

Once back at the island, we used several wooden wheelbarrows to transport the groceries down the boardwalks to the beach house. If the bags were left unattended for too long in between trips, seagulls had to be chased off the week's supplies.

As noted in Mom's preface, in the years before the bridge was built, the fishing crew stayed on the island during the week and lived in the various bunk houses. They usually only went ashore to the mainland on Saturday after the fish was packed out and the boat was cleaned up. With the new bridge access to Captree, the Sunrise had a station wagon, and later a van, with which they transported the crew back to Islip every afternoon. And early every morning they rode in the van from Islip to Captree, returning to the island by skiff.

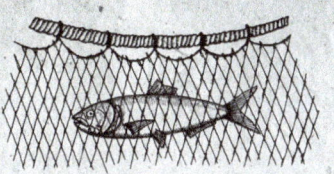

THE CREW

Pieter Schaper

Pieter Schaper, my grandfather, grew up in Zeeland, in Holland. My grandmother was from Friesland, also in Holland. Pieter and his brother, Arie, came to New York through Ellis Island and settled in Sayville, NY, where there was already an established Dutch community.

Pieter started fishing, purchased a schooner that he named *Ebenezer*, and then settled in Nantucket. This is where my father, Louis, was born. My grandfather fished out of Nantucket for a number of years before moving back to the south shore of Long Island. He established the Sunrise Fish Company in Islip, and a fish camp over at Cedar Beach, later moving to Havemeyer Island. It was from there that he started the Sunrise Fish Company pound trap fishery.

In the early 1970s, I sailed into Nantucket for the first time as the young skipper of a 72-foot ketch, *Golden Eagle*. Moored at the Nantucket Boat Basin, I walked up the dock and came across a small shed with the door open. Above the door was scrawled "The Wharf Rat Club." Inside were several very old men, whittling with pocket knives, smoking pipes, relaxing on wooden chairs and an old sofa. I stuck my head in … tried to be friendly … said "hello …" and was greeted by a scowl.

"Who are you?" one of the octogenarians growled.

"Well, I just sailed in—my father was born here—my grandfather used to fish from Nantucket …" I stammered.

"What's yer name boy?"

"Schaper …"

"Schaper!? Your grampa wasn't Pete Schaper, was he?" the old fisherman questioned.

"Yes, that's right, Pieter Schaper—had a schooner—the *Ebenezer*."

"Why … Captain Pete Schaper …" he chuckled, "smartest Dutchman I ever knew!"

"Why … one winter it was so cold; the entire harbor froze up—no one could get in or out. But that crazy Pete Schaper—he got his boat up on skids on top of the ice, raised the sails and sailed across the ice to open water. He went out and got a boatload of fish, and he got top dollar 'cause no other boats could get out to fish!"

This amazing story stayed with me for years, though I wasn't sure if it had any truth to it. A more recent conversation with a lifelong Nantucket resident gave some credence to the tale when he told me that, back in the day, it was common to haul boats out of the water on skids. And he had heard of people skidding them over the ice to open water … so it just could be so.

Grandpa Pete Schaper's Ebenezer *on the East River after unloading his fish at New York's Fulton Fish Market.*

The four Schaper brothers - Nick, Arie, Lou and Bill

Nicholas Schaper (Uncle Nick) was the oldest of Pieter Schaper's sons. I recall Uncle Nick being obsessed with all things mechanical. One year when I was maybe 7 years old, I went with Uncle Nick to take the scow from the island across the bay to Islip. Just the two of us. In my world, the scow was the biggest boat anywhere. As a "scow," it was basically rectangular in shape, about 55 feet long and 25 feet wide, with a bow that angled down. It had a flat shear, the bow being about 5 feet off the water, tapering down to the stern which was only 18 inches above the water. The forward deck was a large open working area with two large Sampson posts up forward. There was a large 5-foot square hatch located just forward of the mast bench. The mast bench was comprised of massive wooden beams and contained the keel-stepped mast, and supported the forward and aft booms.

The mast was an enormous solid wooden spar measuring 24 inches in diameter. It soared 60 feet above the water. The mast was supported by four ¾ inch galvanized steel wire-rope shrouds which led to large turnbuckles anchored by steel chain plates at the edges of the deck. The booms were also solid wood, 14 inches in diameter by 64 feet long. The bottom ends of the booms were clad with a steel housing ending in a swivel gooseneck allowing them to be raised and lowered as well as turned from side to side. At the top end of the booms was another steel housing masthead fitting with tangs and rings for the attachment of the 4-part block and tackle which led to similar fittings at the top of the mast. The 4-part block and tackle was rigged with one-inch manila line which led down the mast to huge cleats on the mast bench. To raise or lower the booms, this line was run from the cleat back to the powered winch drum in front of the wheel house.

Between the wheel house and the mast bench was the winch assembly. The winches consisted of 3 large steel spools which were wound with oiled wire rope. The wire rope was led through large diameter blocks, then through spliced line thimble guides up the boom, and then through a block at the top end of the boom. The wire rope terminated in a large forged steel hook. Any loads to be lifted were secured to the hook with a line or "strap." A strap was heavy line, usually nylon, spliced together in a continuous loop. Straps were used frequently for lifting nets, leaders and poles. The forward winch controlled the single hook on the aft boom. The two aft winches were for the port and starboard hooks on the forward boom.

Setting Leaders

My dad, Louis, running the scow winches.

The winches were operated with 3-foot-long brass hand clutch levers and 4-foot-long counter-weighted foot operated brake levers. These controls were on the starboard side. Despite layers of black paint and oil, the ends of the levers were bright shiny brass from frequent use.

On the port side, the winches had steel covers over the open gears which drove the winches. Those covers saved me from being mangled when, as a kid, I fell off the top of the wheelhouse onto the winches while I was watching my dad operate them during a net copper painting process. My dad immediately stopped the winches and scooped me up with his copper paint covered hands. Aside from a lot of grease and copper paint all over me, I was okay—and thankful for those gear guards!

Outboard of the gears were two 16-inch diameter iron winch drums for hauling on lines.

The winches were powered by the scow's port engine through a power take off assembly run through a truck transmission, which then led to a large sprocket which turned a heavy chain, and then up through the deck to the winch input. When running, it had a great combination of sounds: shafts running through gearboxes, bearings whining, and the clacking sound of an oily chain over sprockets.

By today's standards of cranes, it was indeed primitive. But it worked and it was powerful. For many years it was often called on for tasks outside of fishing operations. Local boats that had been holed and were sinking were lifted up out of the water for repairs with the scow. Several times the Long Island Lighting Company called my dad to use the scow to lift and repair the electric cable that ran under the bay supplying power to Fire Island. When a Hollywood movie studio was filming the Cuban refuge movie *Popi*, starring Alan Arkin, they used the scow for generators, lights, cameras and support.

But back to Uncle Nick … Before they were replaced by a pair of 6-71 Detroit Diesels, the scow was powered by two big Perkins gasoline engines. Uncle Nick was forever fussing over these engines. For some reason, on this particular day, it was only me and Uncle Nick aboard for a several hours run across the bay. The scow, of course, had no autopilot … just some eye splices in a couple of pieces of six-thread that could be looped over the spokes of the steering wheel to hold the helm straight. The steering wheel was a huge wooden relic that turned a drum wrapped with one-inch manila line. Those lines led through holes in the wheelhouse floor, through a system of pulleys, and eventually to the twin rudder quadrants back under the fantail. Needless to say, it was not very responsive and not that easy for a 7-year-old to turn. Heck, standing on a wooden milk crate, I could barely see out the windows, let alone steer.

But that is what I did.

Setting Leaders

"Ronny, take the wheel—I gotta go check the engines."
"But Uncle Nick! Where do I go?!"
"See that buoy way out there? Steer for it."
"Oh … okay. Which side of it?"
"Just go straight for it—try to run it down."

With those instructions, Uncle Nick climbed down into the engine room, which was located just behind and open to the wheelhouse. The Perkins engines were roaring away and I was doing my best to stay on a straight course to the buoy. Uncle Nick liked to take pliers and open a petcock on the top of each of the engine cylinders to evaluate the loud bang bang of the cylinder firing. It sounded like gunshots and didn't help to ease my anxiety as we got closer to the buoy. I often turned around and glanced down to see if he was yet done fiddling with the engines.

"Uncle Nick! We're getting close to the buoy! Which side should we go on?"

He was busy. He didn't want to be bothered.

"Just run it down!"

Hey, I was seven. I hadn't yet learned *red right even returning* and stuff. I just knew buoys marked shallow water and I was steering the biggest boat I knew right at a buoy or the flats!

"UNCLE NICK!!!!!"

Well, he finally came up out of the engine room calmly wiping his hands on a rag. The manila line creaked on the drum as he turned the helm a bit to port narrowly passing the buoy on the starboard side.

In later years, when the Sunrise Fish Company built large freezers at the Islip facility, Uncle Nick obsessed over the compressors. The compressor room was like being in the engine room of a ship. There were several large ammonia compressors run by multiple horsepower electric motors powered though large numerous sheave V-belts. There were huge condensers bolted to the walls. Everywhere were large analog pressure gauges, electrical meters and so on. The compressor room and the workbench there were always spotlessly clean and painted. The tools hanging behind the workbench were outlined, showing where each one should be.

The compressor room.

By the door was a special case containing an ammonia gas mask if needed in an emergency. I am told that in the early days, Uncle Nick had a cot in the compressor room and slept there monitoring "his babies." He also later suffered from emphysema, attributed to ammonia inhalation … and being a heavy smoker.

Setting Leaders

Uncle Arie

Uncle Arie was the second oldest of the Schaper brothers. His usual role was skippering the pound boat and operating the winch to haul the fish aboard. When the scow was required, he skippered it and ran its winches. As previously mentioned, Uncle Arie and Aunt Kate had a lovely beach house with a wraparound enclosed porch overlooking the bay. The walls and ceiling were decorated with a huge array of glass, plastic, wood and cork fishing buoys, and elaborate fishing lures that Uncle Arie had collected over the years after finding them snagged in the pound nets. Each one had a story.

I recall many pleasant evenings on Kate and Arie's porch, watching the lighthouse showing the way to nighttime boaters, listening to Uncle Arie's stories as he puffed away on his pipe … "Then there was the time we were headin' out the inlet and came upon a man's body on the tide." Our young ears perked up with wide eyes in the dim light—hanging on every word. "We pulled a sharpie alongside him. He had been in the water a while—no shirt—slumped forward—just his back and shoulders showin'—and was pretty rank. The boys passed a burlap bag under his arms and, as they pulled him into the sharpie, a couple of eels slithered out from a hole by his stomach."

Following a few health issues, Uncle Arie slowed down on his fishing schedule. He ran the pound boat to raise the traps in the mornings but then would be off when the boat returned to the beach by noon.

Later, with a Coast Guard license, he worked for Bob Federico running daytime excursion and moonlight sail charter boats out of Captree. I sailed many trips with him as mate aboard these boats, which gave me a lot of time to really get to know and love him.

One of these excursion boats was a big steel tub of a boat, the *Captree Mist*. This was a Blount built boat, about 65 feet long with a single Detroit Diesel engine. On moonlight sails we'd navigate channels well known to us along Fire Island. Sometimes we'd slowly loop back and forth several times past the Fire Island Lighthouse … and we had comments from passengers; "Gee Captain, I didn't know there were so many lighthouses along this coast!"

Some nights heavy fog would set in. While we had radar, rather than stressing over safely navigating through the channels, we would slowly push our steel bow up on the Farm Shoals sand bar and "park" for a while. With the engine running, music playing, people partying and zero visibility, no one knew or cared that we weren't moving. When the charter time was over … or the fog cleared … we would back off the sand bar and continue on our way.

A big tubby single screw boat like this can be a little awkward to handle. Our dock space at Captree Boat Basin had us bow in right in front of the main concession building, with a metal ticket vending booth right at the edge of the dock. To approach this slip, three turns had to be made in a sort of S curve to come alongside the pier. The final turn required a burst of engine power in forward with the rudder hard over to starboard to bring the stern in, then an immediate shift into reverse with a strong burst of engine power to stop the boat. Uncle Arie had expertly performed this maneuver hundreds of times.

But … there was one time, on the final gear shift into reverse, when a clevis pin on the shifting cable in the engine room had, unbeknownst to us, fallen out, leaving the transmission in forward gear. When Uncle Arie gave the final engine acceleration to stop the boat, we actually lurched ahead in forward, smashing our high steel bow several feet into the wooden dock ahead! Rose, in the ticket booth nearly got knocked down. Dozens of passengers onboard, who were standing in line for the gangway, fell down like bowling pins. I quickly secured a few dock lines while Uncle Arie shut down the engine.

Fortunately, no one was hurt. The bow of the boat suffered only a dent and some scraped paint. The dock needed repair, but it was not terrible. I suppose these days, there would be numerous lawyers involved. For me, the worst of it was seeing dear Uncle Arie so upset. Who wouldn't be distressed by being captain of a boat that just crashed into a dock with a boatload of people aboard?! We later investigated the engine room and found the clevis pin that had come loose from the transmission linkage. Checking this became part of our daily engine routine.

One of the other boats we used for moonlight sails was the old wooden classic *Point O' Woods IV.* This boat was also about 65 feet long, had two decks for guests and a small wheelhouse up forward. Often guests would bring music to be played over the boat's audio system. This was the era of reel-to-reel tape. These music tapes were on reels about 8 inches in diameter and could play for several hours. The tape player was in a locker on the aft bulkhead of the wheelhouse.

On one occasion when a group of guests came aboard for a party, the lady who had organized it provided us with a reel of tape that she said she had been working on for months. It contained all of their favorite music. We put her tape on the machine, threaded the end into the take-up reel, pressed the rubber securing knobs on the spindles in the center of the reels, started her music playing and closed the locker door. We got the boat under way and everything was perfect.

At night, the wheelhouse was completely dark, except from the glow of the compass and engine instruments. Lights were kept off to preserve night vision on the water. Several hours into the evening, we sensed something on the floor in the wheel house where we had been standing watch. With a small flashlight we were horrified to discover that we were standing knee deep in music tape from the machine! While the music was still merrily playing away, apparently the rubber knob on the spindle of the take-up reel had been jammed by the closed door of the locker. So, as the tape played, it slithered out under the door of the locker onto the dark floor of the wheelhouse instead of being wound up on the reel.

Uncle Arie and I looked at each other, *What do we do now?*

Uncle Arie, a man of quick action, took out his pocket knife, cut the tape, scooped up a couple of armfuls of tape, looked left and right, and pitched the tape overboard! And the music played on!

Even with the vigor of a teenager, working excursion sails all day from early in the morning, then doing moonlight sails sometimes until midnight, I often needed a break. The *Point O' Woods IV* had a nice engine room. I could stretch out comfortably in the space between the twin Cummins diesels and get a little rest. If Uncle Arie needed me he would just rev up and down the throttle of one of the engines and I would go up on deck to take care of business. (This practice plus time spent in the engine room of the pound boat may have contributed to some diminished hearing acuity … WHAT DID YOU SAY?!)

Uncle Bill was the next oldest of the Sunrise Fish Company brothers. Uncle Bill ran the shore-side business end of the fish company. When the pound boat raised the traps, they would radio in to Uncle Bill in Islip with an estimate of what variety and how many pounds of fish they were bringing in. At this time, they were using a "private" VHF radio that only communicated between the station on the boat and one in Islip. Previously they had used the more common AM or double-sideband radios, where anyone listening could hear their conversations. They found that a number of sportfishermen were upset that the commercial boats were catching all the fish and not leaving any for them!

Bill and Arie developed a few code words for the species and quantity of fish to get around this issue—but it was awkward. So, that's why they switched to the proprietary VHF radio to ensure privacy.

"Hey Bill, we got 50 boxes a small medium blues—about 30 boxes a large—30 boxes a timble eye—over."

A "box" was 100 pounds. These were the old pine wood boxes that the crew would nail together over the cold winter nights when there was no fishing. The rectangular box measured 18¼ inches wide by 12 inches high and 30 inches long. When fish were sent ashore from the pound boat in wire baskets, they were dipped into a large wooden tub to wash them, then put upon a Detecto balance arm scale for weighing. The weight of the basket was pre-adjusted on the scale's balance arm so the net weight would be 50 pounds. Fish were added or removed to meet the correct weight. The bottom of the fish box was covered with a few shovelfuls of crushed ice; the fish were layered in, followed by more ice, then the final 50 pounds of fish, followed by a final layer of ice. Then the wooden top of the box would be fitted and nailed on (by hand with a hammer).

Six 100-pound boxes would comprise a pallet, which would be brought by forklift to a refrigerated holding room (the cooler), or to a waiting truck to be taken to market; usually the Fulton Fish Market in New York City.

When Uncle Bill had a tally of the day's catch, he would immediately be on the telephone to his wholesalers, vying for the best price. Typically, pound trap-caught fish commanded a premium price in the market because they were caught alive, were immediately iced, and were sent to market the same day they were caught. Other fishing vessels might be at sea for a week or more. Fish brought up in trawlers' nets were most often dead when they were brought aboard, and then they languished on ice for days before being delivered to market.

Sunrise Fish also supplied many local restaurants with fresh fish on a daily basis which were delivered by a Sunrise pickup truck along with bushels of clams and boxes of frozen shrimp.

My dad, Louis Schaper

Louis, born in Nantucket, was the youngest of the Schaper brothers. Except for a brief stint in the Navy during WWII, Dad fished as soon as he graduated from high school. Before Uncle Arie retired, Dad directed the crew in raising the traps, and operated the large bailing net to scoop the fish from the trap. After Arie retired, he continued to do those jobs and he skippered the pound boat.

There was one particularly memorable day when I was 10 years old. My brother Bob (age 12) and I were out on the pound boat to fish with our dad. As usual, when we reached the fish trap, the pound boat was secured, the two sharpies were manned, and they proceeded to raise the traps.

Lou, Bob and Sandy hoisting the net from the sharpie. Note the line leading down to the block and aft to the winch.

The sharpies each had a gasoline powered (no muffler!) winch mounted amidships. To raise the traps, the two sharpies, on either side of the trap, would start by lifting the net from the inshore side of the pocket. The bowman in the sharpie would use his gaff to hook onto the downhaul line at the tall pole then pass the line to the aft man who would loop the line through a heavy galvanized steel snatch block on the thwart. From there, turns were made around the line-polished brass winch drum. This line led from the winch, through the snatch block, up to the top of the pole (maybe 35 feet above the water) where it was the up-haul line of a four-part block and tackle. The lower end of this block and tackle was underwater where it was attached to a lower corner of the pocket section of the net. Each corner of the net was weighted down with a chain of "gumdrops." These were cast iron weights shaped like the candy gumdrops they were named after. On these pocket corners, the weight usually totaled a couple hundred pounds. Added to this was the weight of all the wet netting and line. All together, these pocket pole lines had to lift close to a thousand pounds. Therefore, the strain on the downhaul line was easily hundreds of pounds.

When the blocks were pulled together, called "two blocked," the bowman would wrap a nipper line, also attached to the thwart, with a back hitch on the downhaul line to secure it while the aft man made the line fast to the pole with a series of back hitches and then tied the coiled line to the pole. Then, they proceeded to the next pole for the same process. There were eight pocket poles, four on each side.

Bob and I were watching from the pound boat as the net was being raised up. As the area within the pocket was slowly reduced, the fish inside excitedly swam around in tighter circles. My dad and Sandy, working the west side of the trap, had already raised two of the pocket pole lines. When they were almost all the way up with the third one, and near maximum strain was on the line … like a gunshot the galvanized steel snatch block broke loose from the thwart and hit my dad on the right side of his forehead! I saw this happen!

He fell to his knees in the sharpie holding his head.

I screamed out to Uncle Arie, "My dad's been hurt!"

Arie called, "You alright Lou?"

My dad waved his right hand, blood running down his arm and off his elbow.

Sandy, thoughtfully, used his gaff to pick my dad's hat up out of the water, then pulled the sharpie alongside the pound boat.

Amazingly, Dad did not lose consciousness. He was helped aboard the pound boat by the crew. One of the crew, Bobby Auer, took charge in trying to make Dad comfortable seated on the aft deck. He used a shirt to apply pressure to the wound to control the bleeding.

My brother and I were in shock.

Uncle Arie immediately gave orders to leave the sharpies and untie the pound boat. He fired up the Detroit Diesel 6-71 and, for the first time ever, gave it full wide-open throttle. Black smoke belched from the smoke stack as the engine roared and the pound boat tried to make its best speed to the Fire Island Inlet.

Uncle Arie called Uncle Bill on the radio, telling him to alert the Coast Guard. Again, this radio could only communicate with the one in Islip—it could not directly call the Coast Guard or other boats for help.

As we approached the Fire Island sea buoy, a fast 41-foot US Coast Guard patrol boat rendezvoused with us. The Coast Guard crew came aboard the pound boat with a metal litter, lifted Dad into it and transferred him to the Coast Guard boat. At full speed they blasted down to Captree Boat Basin where they were met by an ambulance. A quick trip across the Captree Bridge brought Dad to Southside Hospital where he was rushed to surgery.

The surgeon later reported that he was puzzled by the numerous small shiny flecks around the wound and on Dad's face … only to be told that they were fish scales!

Dad had a fractured skull. The surgeon removed bone fragments nearly touching but not impinging upon his brain. After some healing time, a metal plate the size of a silver dollar was implanted in his forehead.

A few months later … Dad was back fishing!

Lou, Arie, and Ward mending a net.

Setting Leaders

Ward Apgar started working for my grandfather at Sunrise Fish Company when he was 14 years old. He continued fishing and working at the Sunrise until well into his 60s. He had a tough demeanor but a heart of gold. He had collected many stories over the years about fishing, people and storms.

Ward was on the island when the famous 1938 hurricane came through. He told of having to climb on the roof of the big net shed to avoid the rising waters ... where he described seeing houses floating down the State Boat Channel.

Like many fishermen, he smoked a lot of cigarettes and loved his beer. His comment on a hot summer day: "It's good beer drinking weather!" On a rainy day: "Gotta have rain to get beer!" And when toasting his first beer of the day: "Here's how!"

Lou and Ward

Ward was always my dad's right-hand man. He could and would do anything. He literally knew the ropes—and how to mend nets, splice and whip lines, handle the sharpies and clean fish. No one could keep up with Ward gutting bluefish.

Sandy Constantine

Sandy Constantine, another long-time Sunrise fisherman, was from Nova Scotia. He was short in stature, quiet, reclusive, almost gruff, but had a rarely used beguiling smile. He and his wife, Agnes, had an old beach house on nearby Captree Island. Early in the morning he would row over in his tiny sharpie with his lunch box and thermos to join the pound boat. In his early years he had crewed in sailing ships hunting seals in Nova Scotia. Perhaps that's where he picked up his love of Copenhagen chewing tobacco which he packed in his lower lip, pausing occasionally to spout out a disgusting spew of brown juice. (This same Copenhagen was once stuffed up my nose as I was hung upside down in the big net shed in retaliation for some prank I had pulled.)

"Hey Mary ... you got any clam chowda?" was one of Sandy's usual pleas to my mom—who had a reputation for the best clam chowder—and often provided Sandy with a well appreciated portion.

As kids, we marveled at how Sandy washed some of his clothes. He would simply tie a line on them and let them tumble in the wake of the pound boat. A quick rinse with fresh water (if that!), dry them on a line, and he was good to go!

Setting Leaders

Bobby Auer—While Bobby was not a long-time employee, to me he stood out not only for the care he gave my dad when he was injured, but because he seemed much more studious, dare I say intelligent, than the usual fishing boat crew. Aside from my brother Richard, I think he was the only crew member I can recall reading books on the pound boat when the work was done.

Fuzzy—I'm not sure how Fuzzy got this nickname … but it could have had something to do with his brain power. He was missing most of several fingers on his hands, he had scars on his arms and face, and his eyes were especially disfigured. I was told that he was building a pipe bomb in his garage … and it went off.

Despite these physical characteristics, he was strong and a good worker, and had a good sense of humor. He gave me the moniker "shark bait" following the well-aimed, crushed ice snowball I directed his way as he was relieving himself off of the aft rail.

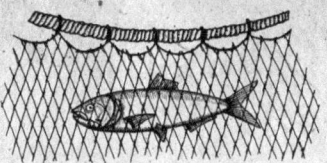

The Fishing Boats

A successful pound fishing operation requires a small fleet of specialized boats.

The Scow, described previously in my trip with Uncle Nick, was built in the early 1920's with heavy solid scantlings. She was a typical "scow" design, with a flat cross-planked bottom, square bow and raised aft bottom for the twin propellers and rudders. Her wide beam provided the stability needed for the loads lifted by her booms.

Most of the time the scow, which was rarely referred to by its name, *Sunrise I*, was tied to the end of the dock as shown in this photo. It was such a fixture there that on the rare days it left the dock, things seemed out of place. When the pound boat came in from its daily offshore trips to the nets, it docked alongside the scow, securing up against a pair of large truck tires used as fenders. Families came to greet the pound boat by walking across the scow like it was a floating dock.

Sunrise I *(the scow)*

Setting Leaders

As teens, we sometimes rigged the scow's aft boom so we could swing out over the water for some acrobatic swimming fun. We would ease the block and tackle on the starboard aft boom stay and haul the boom forward with the port stay so that the top of the boom extended way out over the water. With a large pipe wrench for leverage, the drive shaft to the winches was turned just enough to release the brake pawl on the aft hook. The hook was removed from its deck ring and we'd hand turn the winch drum until the hook was at just the right height for swinging off the scow's engine room deck house. The winch brake was secured ... and the fun began.

With practice, we learned to hold on to the hook, push off from the deck house, swing out 50 feet and up about 10 to 15 feet off the water, then pull up, pivot around and execute a dive off the hook!

Of course, the scow's real purpose was heavy lifting—and there is a lot of that in the fishing business. The scow was needed to pump the poles that supported the nets in the ocean, and to "change" the nets and leaders. How often they needed renewing depended upon water conditions and temperatures, which determined how much sea growth weighed down the nets.

As the scow was not built for rough seas and working the rig required calm waters, the crew had to wait for settled weather to have a "scow day."

All wooden boats, especially old ones that spend most of their days placidly tied to a dock, twist and "work" in a seaway. The stresses of lifting with the booms, plus the side loading on the hull combined with the action of the waves would cause the boat to leak. Under the "counter," that is, under the aft deck, the bottom curved upward to accommodate the twin propellers and rudders. Enormous stresses were placed on this area, which was quite prone to leaking after a tough day of working offshore.

My dad carried a wooden barrel of saw dust onboard to address this issue. Using a long-handled crab net lined with window screen, he would fill the net with saw dust, then sweep the net under the stern of the scow. The saw dust, being buoyant, would float up under the boat and get sucked into the leaking seams. The saw dust would swell up from absorbing water and effectively seal the leaks within a few hours.

The new pound boat, the Sunrise III, *in Islip at the Sunrise Fish plant.*

The Pound Boat—The old pound boat, *Sunrise II*, followed by the new and improved *Sunrise III*, were purpose built for fishing the pound traps.

The *Sunrise III* was built at the Sam Jorgensen boatyard in West Sayville. I am not sure what plans, if any, it was built on, but I often heard the fishermen comparing it favorably to the old *Sunrise II*. The newer boat was larger and deeper, with greater carrying capacity. On the old pound boat, they had actually added "side boards" on the gunwales to keep heaped up "swinging deck loads" of fish from falling over the side. (In later years, if a crewman over-filled one of the wire baskets with fish, one of the old timers would often deride them with "you want side boards on that basket?")

I am sure my dad and uncles all provided input to Sam Jorgensen in the design of the new improved pound boat. I can recall as a young boy spending time in the boatyard as it was being built.

Setting Leaders

The Sunrise III *towing the sharpies side by side.*

It was a fairly simple design: about 45 feet overall in length, around 16 feet of beam, a hull depth of around 10 feet with a 5-foot draft. I believe she was cedar lapstreak planked over white oak frames, copper and bronze fastened. The small wheel house was way up in the bow just to port of center. It had room for only one man to stand behind the brass wheel of the hydraulic steering. The throttle for the naturally aspirated Detroit Diesel 6-71 was a chrome-plated lever on the starboard bulkhead. The mechanical Twin Disc clutch was engaged with a large brass lever which ran in a slot on the starboard side. This lever had a beautiful shining brass patina on its end, the part most often gripped by working hands.

In front of the helm was a 6-inch magnetic compass—the only navigational instrument on board. There was a switch for a windshield wiper and one for the air horn. There was also a two-way radio. The forward windshield hinged upward and was usually held up that way by brass wing brackets. The two side windows could be slid open and were protected from breakage by galvanized wire mesh. On the outside starboard side of the wheelhouse were numerous hand gaff hooks stored in the wire mesh. Below that was a 3-foot-long knife rack with a dozen various sized fish knives. There were several well-worn knife sharpening stones stowed in a slot below the knife rack. On the port side of the wheelhouse was a metal covered cooler for the crew's lunch boxes and a couple of dirty looking glass gallon jugs of drinking water.

While the aft end of the wheel house could be closed up with leeboards which slid into a groove, most often it was left open, except when the boat was shut down for the night.

Standing at the helm, it was two small steps down into the forward cabin, which was actually the engine room. The engine was literally a few feet away from the helmsman. With no attempt at sound attenuation … IT WAS LOUD! It was also warm in that cramped engine room, which made it attractive to young kids not used to the cold ocean air. We would sometimes squeeze past Dad's legs to get down below where we could stretch out on the narrow bench on the port side and pull some clothing or lifejackets over our ears to diminish the roar of the diesel. It was warm but noisy.

With the engine in the bow, there was a long drive shaft supported by several pillow bearings that ran almost the length of the vessel. On deck, in some of the thwarts, there were alumite grease fittings connected to copper tubes that extended down by the bilges to lubricate these bearings. On a weekly schedule, Ward would take out a grease gun and give a few pumps to each bearing. As a boy, when I asked what he was doing, he explained that he was greasing the bottom of the boat so we could go faster—a plausible explanation for a kid.

The dry diesel exhaust roar was slightly diminished by a muffler and was directed to the starboard bow by a removable exhaust elbow. This hot elbow had handles welded on each side so gloved hands could remove it when entering the labyrinth of lines as they approached the fish traps. At the beach house, we could usually hear the pound boat coming before we could see it.

On the raised forward deck, just aft of the exhaust, was the winch used for hauling the fish aboard. The winch operated off a power take off on the engine which ran through a heavy chain and sprockets. A nylon line was secured to the winch drum, then went through a snatch block on the starboard rail, then to another snatch block secured to a ring on the deck next to the mast. From there it went up to the end of the boom, through a galvanized steel block, then out to the fish bailing net secured to the end of a 12-foot aluminum pole.

The wooden mast, just aft of the wheel house, was about 8 inches in diameter and only about 8 feet tall. It had to be short enough to fit under the lines when entering the traps. The mast was securely stepped in the keel and supported by the deck and a forward wire rope shroud secured in the bow. A removable stay was set up on the opposite side of the load. Depending upon winds and current, sometimes the net would be port side to, other times starboard side to.

Just aft of the mast, were hatch covers over fish hold number one. Each wooden hatch cover had an inch and a half diameter hole in diagonally opposite corners so fingers could be inserted to lift and open the hatch. Jumping down inside the hold, it had a depth of about 3 feet. With the bluefish run, when standing in the hold, the deck level was near a man's waist—a good height for using the deck as a cutting board when gutting fish.

Sometimes the crew would line this hold with a heavy plastic tarpaulin. When out in the clean ocean waters, they would use the deck pump hose to fill the hold with seawater for the lobster tanks in Islip. There, another pump would transfer the water into the series of refrigerated lobster tanks at the Sunrise Fish Company shop.

Sunrise III

Gutting bluefish aboard Sunrise II *with the forward pen board removed.*

Setting Leaders

Aft of hold number one was a supporting thwart where a "pen board" was secured. There were two pen boards; one between hatch number one and two, and another aft between hatches four and five. These were made of very heavy oak planks 3 inches thick and 3 feet high and they spanned the width of the boat. They had to be lifted into place and were secured between wooden channels at the sides of the boat. These pen boards retained piled up fish from spilling out forward and aft. There was also a midships pen board that was secured to the other boards to keep fish from sweeping from one side to the other as the boat rolled. The pen boards had removable access gates at each lower end to allow fish to be pushed under the boards at a controlled rate.

The center section of the deck of the pound boat had four holds, each enclosed with numerous hatch covers. Depending upon the species and quantity of fish caught on any particular day, the catch could be divided as needed. Proper weight distribution for the boat's trim was also an important element in stowing the fish.

Aft of the pen board was hatch number five, which was often used for stowing the flaked ice. Ice was also stowed in the iceboxes back aft. At the Islip plant, a continuously running ice machine produced ice flakes for chilling the fish. (I recall a crew's revenge for some of the pranks played on them when they held me in the icebox, on top of the ice, when I was wearing only a bathing suit!—Are we seeing a pattern here? I must have been a *very* mischievous fellow in my youth!)

At the aft end of the pound boat were two pairs of heavy steel davits, one on each side. While they were rarely used, there were times when the Fire Island Inlet was so rough, the sharpies had to be hoisted up on the davits, out of the water, because if they were towed behind as they usually were, they could be swamped or sunk. Under normal conditions, the two sharpies were towed side by side, one from each quarter. With a bit more seaway, they would be towed in tandem, using a long nylon towline from the center of the pound boat's transom as seen in the following photo.

The Sunrise III *crossing the bar. Traversing Fire Island Inlet with a swell running, the sharpies were towed well aft and in tandem. Here a breaking wave shows how narrow the channel was.*

This is the old pound boat, the Sunrise II, *circa 1950—note the side boards and davits.*

Setting Leaders

The Sharpies, by definition, were long flat-bottomed boats. These had a pointed bow and transom stern with a notch cut out for the sculling oar. Sculling, which now seems to be a lost art, is when a single oar is moved from side to side and slightly twisted when doing so, to propel a boat forward. My brothers and I had to learn this at an age when the 12-foot-long, 20-pound wooden oar was somewhat intimidating. We always marveled at the speed and agility of Ward sculling his sharpie in the ocean.

Dad sculled his Hyster sharpie to the pole, then pulled in the oar as Sandy gaffed the line.

There were four sharpies in the fleet: two Hyster sharpies (so named for the gasoline powered winch, or Hyster), and two scow sharpies, with no winches. These boats were built by my dad, Louis Schaper, on the floor of the shop in Islip during the winter when there was no fishing. Each was about 16 feet 9 inches long, with a 5-foot 3-inch beam, and 24 inches deep, drawing only about 12 inches of water. They were very sturdily built of fiberglassed ¾ inch marine plywood with numerous oak frames, knee-supported thwarts, and reinforced transoms and bows. All fastenings were made with the finest Everdur bronze screws and bolts. Heavy laminated steam-bent oak gunwale strakes were capped with several strips of half oval 1¼ inch brass rub rails. The bows, stem and stern corners were generously protected with split automobile tires.

In the center of the Hyster sharpies was a single cylinder gasoline engine of about 12 horsepower that powered, through a cast iron gearbox, a brass winch drum. This Hyster motor was protected inside a wooden engine box measuring about 30 inches high, 3 feet long and 2 feet wide. Inside the top lid there was a small cubby containing a coiled up starting pull cord, a spare spark plug and wrench, and a dirty rag. A square 1-gallon copper gas tank was mounted high up in the box. Starting the engine required turning on the gas petcock, pulling out the choke, wrapping the knotted starting pull cord around the flywheel, then giving a mighty pull on the cord. This engine starting process could take a number of tries, sometimes involving replacing the spark plug and *always* involving a fair amount of cursing.

When it finally fired up, IT WAS LOUD! For some reason, these engines did not have mufflers—there was simply a straight 1-inch steel pipe leading directly from the cylinder head out through the side of the engine box.

The brass winch drum extended through the starboard side of the engine box. The work-polished drum was about 10 inches in diameter and a foot long. As described earlier, a line would lead to this drum via a snatch block on the thwart.

Inside the upper bow of each sharpie there was a short crosswise wooden frame called the breast hook. This part strengthened the bow and served as a holder for the hook part of the gaff. Gaffs were carried in all the sharpies and several larger ones were carried on the pound boat. They were constructed of a sturdy 2½ inch diameter wooden pole with a sharpened wrought steel hook on the end. The hook was made of ½ inch diameter steel and was about 5 inches across, terminating in a sharp point. Gaffs were used as boat hooks to grasp lines, the net or the side of the pound boat. When large fish were caught, they were used to gaff or hook the fish.

And, as mentioned earlier, each sharpie also carried a large wooden oar for sculling.

The two scow sharpies did not have the Hyster winches, but were otherwise the same size and construction. My dad built the newest one with a "well" for an outboard motor. About 6 feet from the stern, he built a sort of box arrangement that allowed an outboard motor to be mounted so that the propeller did not extend aft of the transom. This feature was important for working around the nets and was especially useful for running long anchor lines out for securing the scow during its ocean operations.

Net setting operation with the outboard powered sharpie in the foreground.

When not in use, the scow sharpies were usually stowed overhanging the aft deck of the scow. To put one of these boats up there, the aft scow hook was secured to the breast hook to lift it up while the bow line was led to the scow's aft deck winch to pull it forward.

The Hyster sharpies stayed in the water secured in the "sharpie bin" next to the main dock, where the bow lines were tied on posts up in the sand, while the looped stern line was tied off with a becket knot to the pilings of the dock.

The Skiff was a utility boat used to transport the crew across the bay in the old days and, after the bridge was built, to and from Captree Island. While it was usually simply called "the skiff," it was actually named the *Joyce* after one of Uncle Nick's daughters. The lapstreak hull had a narrow bow which would slice through the waves. It was about 23 feet long with a slender beam of only about 8 feet. The boat was completely open with a tiny cabin (or locker) up forward. As small kids, two of us could squeeze in there to get out of the weather or the cool night air. Up on the starboard side was a re-purposed brass fire extinguisher tank which was the expansion tank for the engine's cooling system. The engine was cooled with a simple keel cooler comprised of one-inch copper piping secured to the bottom of the boat. With the engine warmed up, this tank radiated some heat to the small cabin. As a kid, this cramped spot was a favorite warm haven from the chill night air after a family evening swim in the ocean at Fire Island State Park (later named Robert Moses State Park).

The skiff (aka the Joyce*)*

The engine box was located amidships and provided seating for the helmsman and maybe four other passengers. The engine was a venerable Chrysler Crown 6-cylinder gasoline engine. On the forward end of the engine box were the engine instruments: oil pressure gauge, engine temperature gauge, ammeter, and tachometer. The only way to see these instruments was to read them upside down from behind the helm, looking below and between your legs—or to squat forward of the helm and look aft.

Also located on the forward end of the engine box was a manual pull choke, a starter button and a switch to turn on the running lights. On the upper right-hand side of the engine box was a 6-inch-long brass lever for the engine throttle. To the right of the helm was a 2-foot-long brass lever to operate the manual clutch. For some reason, reverse gear was very temperamental and could only be applied very gingerly.

To start the engine, first one lifted up the engine box cover and removed the helmsman's seat pad which was stored on top of the engine—an ancient square boat cushion, rock hard from many years of use. My dad taught me the "trick" to starting this engine: pull out the choke, advance the throttle one quarter, push the start button ... listen for the starter to turn over the engine (three groans), then quickly push the choke all the way in and the engine magically roared to life! The exhaust was a dry muffled stack just aft of the engine box.

The helm was a traditional bronze steering wheel about 14 inches in diameter with wooden handles on the ends of the spokes. There was a small compass on the binnacle by the helm.

Just forward of the helm, the deck stepped down and was crossed by a thwart seat. On the starboard side was a brass cylinder hand pump. This boat's bilges always needed pumping.

Back aft, the stern was decked over a couple of feet forming a closed locker housing the athwart-ships cylindrical gas tank.

Just like all of the other boats in the fleet ... and the net houses ... the skiff was painted Navy grey. I think that Uncle Nick, who had a reputation for buying things in bulk and quantity for better economy, must have bought many gallons of Navy surplus grey paint and, therefore, everything was painted that color. In later years, when the net houses needed a new coat of paint, my mom volunteered to paint them. But she would pick the color! So ... the net sheds went from Navy grey to a brilliant barn red!

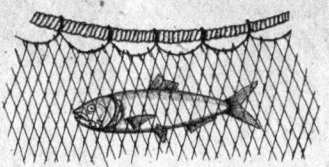

THE FISH TRAPS

The Fish Traps are described as pound nets. A network of leaders, lines and nets were supported by as many as 100 large poles, pumped into the ocean floor. The way pound traps work is; fish generally swim along parallel to the shore, and when they come to an obstruction—in this case, the wall of leader lines blocking their passage—they swim offshore to go around it. As they head offshore, keeping the leaders to one side, they soon have the large mesh webbing of the "heart" section of the trap enclosing them. The "heart" is so named as it is shaped like a heart, and it channels the fish toward the "funnel." Much like any funnel, it compresses and directs the fish ever tighter into the "pocket" section of the trap. The funnel extends well into the pocket, which is nearly round in shape. Once in the pocket, fish swim around and around its circumference, hopefully not discovering the narrow funnel which would be their only way out.

The following article and illustration by EW Gudger (missing a page or two), describing the Sunrise Fish Company's pound trap, appeared in the February 1936 issue of the Journal of Natural History.

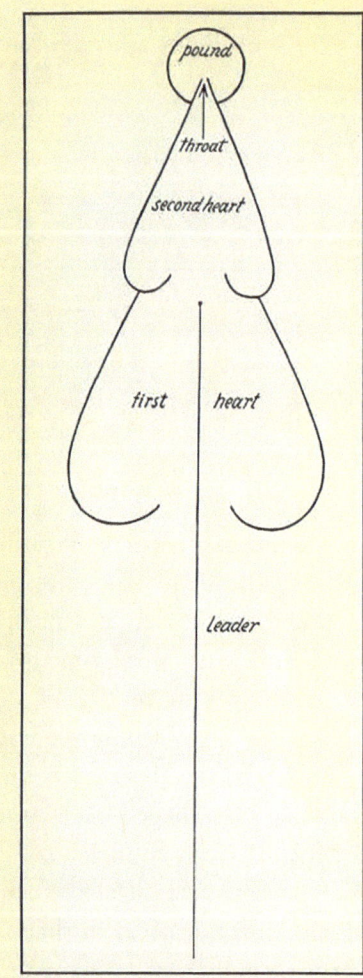

HOW A POUND NET WORKS
This diagram illustrates just how the 1800-foot leader guides the fish until they reach the pocket at the other end. This particular pound trap was perfected by the Schaper brothers, who operate a pound net fishery off Fire Island

is not wooded, the photograph on page 169 of an ordinary pound net will show what the Schapers saw on this memorable morning.

The net that caught the fish

However, the Schapers' pound net is not of the ordinary kind, but is one which is the outgrowth of their experience. Hence it is well here to refer to the drawing on this page and to give a description of their pound net or trap with a brief explanation of how it works.

This huge trap is supported on poles as long as a ship's mast. First there is the 1800-foot "leader" which begins inshore in water 40 feet deep and ends out in water 56 feet deep and everywhere reaches from bottom to surface. This leads into the first "heart," which measures 230 feet around each curve. The first "heart" leads into the smaller second one (195 feet around each curve), and it into the "pound" or pocket. The first heart has at the base on each side of the "lead" openings 60 feet wide and about 50 feet deep, while the "doorway" at the tip is 40 feet wide and 52 feet deep. The second heart opens into the "pound" by a channel which at the base or rear is 15 feet wide by 56 deep, but which narrows to 4 feet wide and 49 feet deep at the front end in the pound. The pocket is a bag 60 feet in diameter and 56 feet deep, suspended on long poles set several feet outside the pocket, so that the net will swing clear of the poles and about two feet above sea bottom. At the tops of the poles are pulleys through which are rove ropes attached to the bottom of the pocket. By these the bottom is brought near the surface so that the captured fish can be easily removed.

Here is how this trap and its parts work. Fishes going east or west along the shore strike the leader and working toward deeper water find their way into the first heart. Their tendency is to still go forward into the second heart and from it into the pocket. The fish seem little inclined to come out through the doorways, but are always nosing against the net. So the whale shark got in and so he behaved.

When, early on August 9, the fishermen reached their net, everything appeared normal, the great fish being invisible. The crew presently began to lift the pocket, working on the "throat" first to close that way of escape for the fishes. When the throat had been hoisted half-way up, the great tail of the huge fish came into view. Arie Schaper from his low (18-foot)

As mentioned earlier, pound trap caught fish often commanded a higher market price because they were landed alive, immediately iced and shipped the same day. Trawlers drag their nets on the bottom. By the time they haul up their nets the fish may have drowned and been pressed hard against the nets

Setting Leaders

for hours, squashing their flesh. The fish were iced down, but trawlers usually stayed out for days or a week at a time, making their fish not nearly as fresh as pound trap fish.

Because the fish were alive, the Sunrise caught the attention of New York's Coney Island Aquarium. The director, Dr. Carleton Ray, contacted my father and asked if they could take a few trips on the pound boat to obtain some specimens for the aquarium. In Islip, they brought aboard several fiberglassed wooden tanks equipped with air hose bubblers and oxygen tanks. Once out in the ocean, the tanks were pumped full of clean seawater. The scientists used long handled nets to scoop up sample fish as they swam around the pocket. When the fish were being bailed aboard, there were pauses when an interesting specimen flapped around the deck catching the attention of one of the scientists who scurried through the hundreds of frantic fish to grab his prize. Numerous fish were placed in the tanks, sustained by the air bubblers.

We were later invited to the Coney Island Aquarium as Dr. Ray's guests where we were given a behind-the-scenes tour. The most memorable part for me was hand feeding a Sunrise-caught mackerel to Olaf, a 1400-pound walrus!

Setting leaders was always the most strenuous back-breaking task involved in preparing the ocean pound nets for the fishing season. While our college chums were off to the beaches of Jamaica or skiing the Rockies for spring break, my brothers and I were pressed into duty helping my dad and uncles, along with the regular fishing crew, with the labor-intensive arrangement of the myriad lines and nets comprising Sunrise Fish Company's pound nets. College kids' soft hands, more used to pencils and typewriter keys, were soon worn red and raw, bleeding from handling coarse rough manila and nylon lines, something the salty old crewmen had built up calluses from long ago.

The ocean pound traps, set off the south shore of Long Island's Fire Island, were arranged with some 80 to 100 "poles." They were called "poles," though they were mostly hickory trees measuring 16 inches in diameter at the base and running 40 to 60 feet in length. As described earlier, these massive logs were hydraulically pumped with a fire hose and pipe arrangement into the sea floor to a depth of about 15 to 16 feet. The inshore water depth, where the leaders started, was around 20 feet. With an offshore water depth of about 60 feet, two poles had to be spliced together to accommodate the greater depth.

Leaders stretched out on the dock for repair. My brother Richard on the left, Ward in the center and Dad on the right.

"The leaders" were multiple strands of ¼ inch diameter line spaced about 10 inches apart, secured to a 1¼ inch diameter top line and bottom line. The 1¼ inch line formed a sort of rectangular frame measuring about 50 feet wide and, depending upon the water depth, between 20 to 50 feet deep. The bottom corners were weighted down with the previously described heavy iron "gumdrop" weights, weighing between 30 and 50 pounds each. In some locations in the traps, such as the corners of the pocket, multiple gumdrops were attached in a series. To attach the gumdrops to the leaders or nets, a steel triangle was spliced onto the bottom lines. Steel connectors called "staples," so named because they looked like crimped staples, were inserted through the center slot in the gumdrop and hooked over the triangle on the line. Additional gumdrops could be added by hooking in another staple. At the bottom of the gumdrop a split circular steel ring would be inserted through the staple and then the split opening was hammered together to secure it.

SETTING LEADERS

Sets of leaders with the "gum drop" weights removed (seen arranged on the edge of the dock). The leaders were hoisted up by the scow's boom and cleaned of sea growth by a high-pressure fire hose, then spread out on the dock to dry and be repaired.

Before "setting" the new leaders, the old sea growth covered ones had to be removed. Out in the ocean, the scow was secured by lines to the poles and by large anchors which were set out by the sharpies. The booms were swung over and the winch hooks made fast to the upper leader lines. The winches hauled the leaders high up out of the water as the gumdrops were hauled on deck. The leaders would be running with dirty water, seaweed and growth that dropped to the deck … and onto the crew. Many times, we could scoop up live seahorses off the deck and save them in a bucket of water. The dirty leaders were carefully stacked in a pile on the deck while a steel wedge was pounded with a heavy hammer to open the split rings to remove the gumdrops so they could be used on the new clean leaders. Once these were secured, the real back-breaking part of setting leaders began. A replacement set of newly copper-painted leaders was aboard the scow to set in place of the ones that had been removed.

The end of each new leader was lowered by hand over the side of the scow into the water. While holding up the weight of the gumdrops and the leader itself, you had to walk along the edge of the deck and stretch the top line all the way out to reach each pole. My back hurts now just writing about this! Then each end had to be secured to the poles.

Okay—we got one done. Shift the scow, pull up the anchors (by hand) from the sharpie and set up for the next leader—good—only 12 more sets to go.

This was exhausting work if you were a tough old fisherman used to being in the elements all day doing demanding physical labor. For a college kid, by the end of the day, which you thought would never come, you were beat: sun and wind burned, hands raw, swollen and bleeding, arms, legs and back aching from the unaccustomed exertion.

Finally, when the last leader was set, the anchors were stowed, the sharpies were hauled aboard the aft deck, Dad aimed the scow for the Fire Island Inlet for the 90-minute ride back to the island. Off duty for a good hour, the best place—maybe the only place—to stretch out for a rest, was aft of the pilot house on top of the engine room. This deck house was stacked with salty scratchy fibrous coils of rope—but laying on top of them felt like a feather bed after a day like this.

Sometimes my brother Bob would take some black mussels which he had gathered off the poles, and using long handled pliers from the engine room, he'd hold them, one by one, over the hot diesel engine exhaust to roast them. Now Moules de la Diesel will never make Gourmet magazine, but he thought they were delicious.

While in my *self-centered, home from college, having to work too hard frame of mind*, I never gave a thought to how exhausted Dad must have been. He not only physically worked harder than we tender college kids did, he also had the stresses of performing the very demanding and complex job of directing the crew to do the work required. Now, as we were finally heading in, he had to pilot the overloaded scow back though a sometimes-treacherous inlet, around numerous shoals and dodge other boat traffic. Meanwhile, we were trying to get comfortable for a nap and maybe roast some mussels. What would it have meant to him if I had walked into the wheelhouse and said "Hey Dad, why not let me take 'er for a bit … you can take a break." Why didn't I do that? It would have meant so much to him.

What was Dad thinking about on this solitary run back to the island? The scow wasn't too fast, especially with this load of dirty leaders aboard … so there were not a lot of tricky turns. He was likely thinking: *Let's see … it's 3:45 now … we'll get to the island about 4:20 … the crew will be wanting to get home right away … we can maybe leave washing these leaders till after we're back from the traps in the mornin'... why is that starboard engine running a little hot? I've got to check the bilges when we get in... Ward's Hyster sharpie needs a new spark plug... what's Bobby doing with that engine exhaust?... gotta top off the diesel in the pom boat... wonder what Mary's makin' for dinner?*

I'm sure these and a thousand other thoughts came to Dad's mind as he navigated the scow safely back to the dock while his crew idled and slept. How sweet it would have been for him to get a short break after constantly being "on" since 6 a.m. Sure ... all these years later I think of it.

Dad piloting the scow after a long day on the ocean.

Raising the nets—Every day, except Sunday, the pound boat would approach the offshore side of the pocket. The boom was lowered to the deck and the exhaust elbow was removed to lower the profile for entering under the offshore support lines. Back aft, each sharpie was tended by its bowman; the offshore boat was brought alongside away from the net and the inshore boat was held aft, clear of the pocket. "Nipper lines" forward and aft were passed through round brass thimbles spliced into the top line of the pocket and secured to large bronze cleats at the gunwale. (A nipper line is a short temporary line used to secure a boat or another line.) The offshore support lines that the boat had to duck under were removed from their thimbles on the top line and tied out of the way on the outside of the pound boat.

Hyster sharpie hauling down on a pocket pole to lift the net, concentrating the fish in the pocket. Note how the tall pole is spliced together.

The sharpies were manned with two or three crew: the bowman used his gaff to pull the boat inshore to the first pocket lifting pole; the aft man used his oar to scull, if needed, and to start the noisy gasoline Hyster motor; and sometimes there was a third man to handle the downhaul line from the pole. At the pole, the downhaul line was led through the snatch block on the thwart and then passed aft to be wrapped on the Hyster winch. As the 4-part blocks came up out of the water, they often screeched and squealed with the great weight they were lifting. The bowman would coil up the hoisted line around the bow of the sharpie.

The pocket hauled up. A pair of "gum drop" weights that held each corner of the net open when under water.

Once the net was up, usually just clear of the water surface, the bow or third crewman made a hitch and numerous turns with a nipper line around the downhaul line to hold it and, with a quick nod to the aft man to indicate that he was ready, he spun the line off the winch. The bowman then took a turn with the line around the pole, secured it with a rolling hitch and back hitch, and used a bight of the line to secure the coiled line to the pole. The loaded nipper line was released and the downhaul line snapped against the pole. The bowman then used his gaff to pull the sharpie to the next pole to be hoisted.

This same operation was happening in another Hyster sharpie on the other side of the trap. Each sharpie crew watched their counterpart to ensure that the net was being evenly raised. Delays by any boat were met with taunts from the other sharpie crew to *'move along!'*

As the four pocket pole blocks were raised, the size of the pocket containing the fish became progressively smaller and the fish became more active, splashing and jumping as they were crowded together. From each side the top line of the pocket was temporarily lowered so the sharpies could pull themselves inside the net. Starting from the inshore side, the bowman reached down and hooked the netting pulling it up so the other crew could grab it with their hands. Then began the process called "webbing up." By grasping handfuls of net and sinking their fingers through the mesh, the men, working together, would pull the net up and into the sharpie. As they worked closer to the pound boat, they had to dump the slack net behind them so they could move forward, crowding the fish ever closer together.

The crew "webs up" by pulling the net up over the side of the sharpie, concentrating the fish for the scoop net. Webbing up requires a strong back, mighty arms and fingers like steel claws.

As the fish were bailed, the sharpie crew webbed up tighter to concentrate the fish for easier scooping.

On the pound boat, the boom was hoisted to its full height and the deck winch was engaged. Standing aft, usually Lou or Ward grasped the end of the 2½ inch diameter aluminum pole of the bailing net. Another crewman held the net release line and Arie ran the winch. The winch lifted the scoop net over the side, the pole was pushed into the net under the fish, then the winch pulled up the filled net. The man on the release line pulled the net over the deck then released the line which opened the bottom of the scoop net. Flapping, splashing fish spilled across the deck. Back over the side, the scoop net gathered another load.

Sometimes there was such a quantity brought aboard that the decks were covered several feet deep with jumping fish. Selected hatch covers were removed to allow fish to tumble down into the hold.

Setting Leaders

Heading back to the island, fish being sorted, gutted and iced down. Uncle Arie at the helm, sister Robin up there with him. Left to right: Larry, Ward, Dad, cousin Gary, and back aft, Sandy.

The scoop net was how they landed most of the fish. But there were exciting times when they caught LARGE fish in the net and had to land them without using the scoop net. There were days when they caught as many as a dozen tunas ranging in size from 800 to 1200 pounds each! There once was a 15-foot tiger shark. And one time I saw a large sword fish simply put his bill in the netting and, with two flips of his tail, slash a 5-foot hole in the net and swim away!

To land a big tuna fish, the sharpies would have to go into the net. With the boat's gaff, or using one of the larger gaffs from the pound boat, they would attempt to gaff the tuna near its head as he swam by … and hang on! Several men had to hold onto the gaff while they tried to get additional gaffs in the fish. Tuna are very strong creatures and they fight really hard.

Gaffing a big tuna could be wet and wild for the sharpie crew.

Lou has the tuna on the gaff, Arie assisting; Jimmy Reich and Sandy Constantine standing by.

SETTING LEADERS

Once the tuna's head could be raised, a two-foot-long steel rod with a nylon line spliced to an eye in the end would be passed up through the fish's gills and out its mouth. This line was then pulled with the winch and secured to the stern of the pound boat with the tuna's head out of the water. A long knife was used to cut into the fish's heart to bleed him out. The mad shaking and death throes of these powerful fish shook the entire boat.

Lou and Arie lead a tuna with a line tethered through its mouth and gills, over the top line of the net. The big fish would be secured to the stern of the pound boat until it could be hauled aboard with the power winch.

Dad gaffing a tuna. Note how the net is tensioned as it is hauled up to the poles. A pair of gumdrop weights can be seen hanging down from the lifted net.

Setting Leaders

Hauling a tuna aboard using the boom and winch.

The crew proudly poses with a tuna, its belly packed with ice.

When the tuna was hauled aboard, the crew would use a long knife to cut open the belly and remove the entrails, gutting the fish. Often a hatch board was inserted and twisted to hold the belly open while cleaning it out. The cavity would be washed out with seawater then packed with shaved ice, and then the entire tuna was iced down and covered with canvas.

After all the fish were removed from the nets, the sharpies released the hoisted lines and the straining blocks screeched their way back under water.

Leaving the trap on a calm peaceful day. While days like this made for easier boat work, the fishermen contended that rougher weather produced more fish. 'Ya need a snotty sou'wester t' catch bluefish,' they would say.

The sharpies were tied astern of the pound boat for the one-hour voyage back to the island during which the crew sorted, cleaned and iced the catch. Most of the fish were stowed in the holds below deck and liberally covered with crushed ice. Other species like mackerel or squid were loaded into 55-gallon steel drums on deck. The drums were filled with clean seawater and ice and then covered with canvas.

Setting Leaders

A successful day of fishing was evidenced by how low on her lines the pound boat sat—and by the number of gulls in attendance.

The pound boat approaching the island; the scow in the foreground and Captree State Park in the background.

Late morning, when the pound boat came in from the ocean, it was greeted by family and nearby island folk seeking fresh fish for the dinner table.

One time, when they caught a 15-foot tiger shark with an estimated weight of 1500 pounds, the crew had to literally cut it in half to haul it aboard! In its stomach was the head of a 250-pound tuna fish and the partially digested shell of a turtle. After the shark was gutted and cleaned, we saved the huge head, which was nearly 2 feet across. I iced it down and covered it with burlap to keep it fresh, as I intended to cut out the large jaws later in the day.

After a full day of work ending with packing out the pound boat in Islip, the boat was brought back to the island and I was ready to work on the shark jaws. The fish had been killed at about 8 o'clock that morning. It was around 6 o'clock that evening when I started working on it—so it had been dead for over ten hours. I had at the ready a variety of sharp knives and gaff hooks. I started by using a hand gaff hook in the lower lip and pulled the gaping jaws open, revealing seven rows of triangular razor-sharp teeth. The largest teeth were in the front row and they were 1½ inches long. The rows behind those were progressively smaller. I understood that when a front tooth broke off, a replacement tooth would fill in from the next row.

With one hand I held the jaws open using the hand gaff, and with my other hand I started cutting around the jaws with a sharp knife. Near the hinge are the powerful muscles that close these mighty jaws. Just as I inserted my knife into the muscle—SNAP! The jaws slapped shut with such speed and force it pulled the gaff hook out of my hand. The sound was like slamming shut a large suitcase. I jumped back like it was about to chase me around the deck!

When I had calmed down … and counted all of my fingers … I thought about what had just happened. Sure, the shark was dead alright—but, because it had been iced down all day, the muscles were still "alive." I recalled my high school science class where we made the dead frog's leg jump by touching it with electrodes from a battery: Galvanic reaction. So, it may have been the salt water covered, steel blade of the knife that had imparted a jolt to the shark's jaw muscle giving me a good scare.

I finally cut the jaws out of the head. They were so big that I could step right through them. I buried them in the sand by the shore to let the little creatures there clean them off.

Tiger shark jaws.

But that tiger shark was certainly not the biggest fish caught by the Sunrise Fish Company. That title is in the lore of the Schaper family and indeed recorded in Long Island maritime history. I am referring to the 1935 landing of a 35-foot, 8-ton whale shark! What started as a normal day of fishing turned into one of excitement and fame for the Schaper brothers.

Whale sharks, the world's largest true fish (they are neither in the whale nor the shark family) are typically only found in tropical waters, so it was unusual to find one so far north. This one got tangled up in the nets and, being unable to propel itself and move water through its gills it, unfortunately, drowned. It was a big project to remove the beast from the nets and, with all the winches on the scow working, haul it aboard on the starboard side.

The scow on the way in from the ocean with the whale shark on deck.

The scow brought the whale shark into Islip where throngs of visitors paid to see this large unusual catch.

Area newspapers carried the story, sending crowds of people to the Islip dock. Soon the summer sun was making the fish smell, so the crew went to a local funeral home and got some formaldehyde to pour over it. Eventually William K. Vanderbilt purchased the carcass, had a taxidermist preserve it and placed it in his private collection. The Schaper brothers' whale shark may still be viewed suspended from the ceiling at the Vanderbilt Museum in Centerport on Long Island. It is said to be the world's largest taxidermied fish.

The whale shark on the scow in Islip.

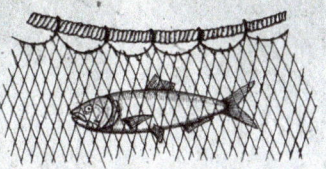

The Fish

While the whale shark, tuna and tiger shark made for some excitement, it was the seasonal runs of market fish that paid the bills.

Bluefish arrived in the summer time and were one of the more lucrative catches. When the blues came aboard, they were quickly iced down and covered with tarps. Then all hands got busy gutting and sorting them for size.

Standing in the holds cleaning bluefish.

The tiniest bluefish are called snappers. As kids, we loved snapper fishing and would prepare by first catching some shiners (also called spearing)—which we used for bait—with either a small seine net, or with what we called a screen. A seine net is a fine mesh netting, usually about 4 feet deep, with lead weights spaced along the bottom to hold it down, and cork floats on the top line to hold it level with the surface of the water. A broomstick or pole was secured to each end. The length varied, but ours was about 30 feet long. We would walk along the shore looking for schools of shiners. One person, holding the pole, would drag one end of the net off the beach out to waist deep water while the other end was held on the beach. The offshore end would be circled around (usually up current) and then maneuvered to close in on the beach. If any other kids were around, they would splash the water in front of the net as it neared the shore to deter the fish from swimming out ahead of the seine.

Both ends of the net were pulled together on the beach sand, making sure that the lead line and float lines were evenly pulled so no fish escaped either under or over the net. The catch was pursed together, making the net into a sort of bag, and then dumped into a bucket with a few inches of seawater. Aside from the targeted shiners, there was always an interesting variety of "by catch." There would be small billed eels, various crabs, killies, and other types of small fish, along with gobs of seaweed. Most of these were examined and released to live another day.

Setting Leaders

Smaller quantities of bait could be caught with a screen. This was a simple 18-inch square of window screening (from the machine shop loft) formed around a stiff copper wire frame. Twine was tied to each corner and secured in the center to a lifting line. A small bit of copper wire inserted in the middle of the screen was used to hold a crushed crab, starfish, or even a bit of bread for bait. The screen was lowered down into the water, waiting for the shiners to find the bait. When a good number of fish attacked the bait, the screen was quickly pulled up with the line, capturing a handful of shiners.

Our favorite spot for snapper fishing was off the end of the jetty. It was such a good spot that it attracted the attention of none other than Robert Moses, who had the captain of his motor yacht tie off to the jetty next to us. We didn't mind—he gave us cookies and cold drinks! Of course, as a kid at that time, we didn't know what a political giant he was.

The end of the jetty was our favorite spot for snapper fishing.

After catching a good string of snappers (we would run twine through the gills and out their mouths, leaving the line hang in the water to keep them cool), we would scale, gut and cut off the heads. Mom would roll them in flour, and soon they were sizzling in butter in the cast iron skillet on the stove.

These were our snappers—ranging in size from 4 to maybe 9 inches long. On the pound boat, "snapper blues" were between 12 and 18 inches long. The next larger size was "small medium," then "medium," next "large," and finally "jumbo." Market prices were usually best for the medium sizes. Bluefish have razor sharp teeth. When they were bailed aboard the pound boat, they jumped and snapped, sometimes finding and making unwary fingers bleed.

Mackerel would often run in the fall of the year. There are numerous varieties of mackerel. The kind most often caught in the pound nets were the thimble-eye mackerel (called "timble eyes" by the fishermen); also called cub mackerel. In lesser quantities, they also caught the larger Boston or Atlantic mackerel.

The mackerel were usually packed in brine in wooden barrels to ship to market. They were packed "in the round," which means they were not cleaned or gutted. On the pound boat they would be put into the ubiquitous cut off 55-gallon steel drums, filled with ice and seawater. Once at the dock in Islip, they were sent ashore in baskets, weighed and then packed in wooden barrels. These barrels were prepared by lining the bottom with about 4 inches of coarse salt, then a few shovelfuls of crushed ice, then a basket of mackerel, more salt, more ice and so on until the measured weight was made and the barrel was full. The barrel would be sealed with water tight canvas secured with a steel barrel hoop, then hammered down tight.

The salt was packaged in 100-pound bags. These were stored upstairs away from the damp air in the shop. I recall Tommy, a big powerfully built Black man who looked like a prizefighter, carrying one of these bags over his shoulder and another one under his arm, effortlessly descending the narrow wooden stairs carrying 200 pounds of salt!

Mackerel were also frozen and shipped throughout the United States to zoos and aquariums for feeding the animals.

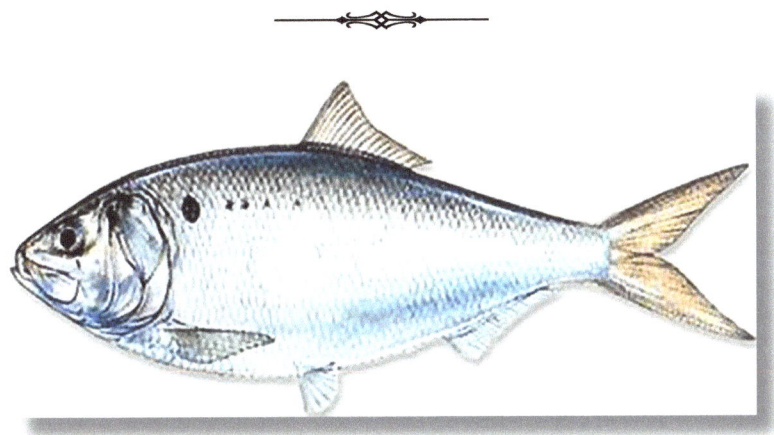

Bunkers, also called menhaden, pogy, or mossbunker, are an extremely oily fish, used by the earliest colonists as fertilizer for their crops. They usually travel in huge densely packed schools and support a very large fishery, providing fish oil and meal for agricultural and industrial uses.

Bunkers caught in the pound traps were used mostly for recreational bait, both as whole fish and also ground into chum. At the Sunrise dock in Islip, whole bunkers were placed in galvanized steel pans or sometimes waxed cardboard trays, each holding about 40 pounds of fish. The pans or trays were slid onto the coils in one of several "blast freezers." The temperature in these large rooms was well below zero and, with powerful fans circulating the frigid air, the fish would freeze solid in a matter of hours. Later, the panned bunkers were dunked in a water tub, popped out of the pan and stacked on pallets before returning them to the huge storage freezer. The cardboard trays were also stacked on pallets and put into frozen storage. Most of these were sold to wholesale bait companies.

Trays of bunkers in the blast freezer.

Trays of frozen bunkers.

When there was a large catch of bunkers, the bunker chum operation was set up and the pound boat was moved to the north end of the Islip dock, adjacent to the large industrial meat grinder. This heavy-duty cast iron machine stood about 7 feet high and was powered by a huge 240-volt electric motor. The bunker chum grinding began when the pound boat crew rigged a conveyor belt hopper into an aft hold. Bunkers were shoveled into the conveyor to lift them off the boat. They were then dumped into the hopper of the next conveyor belt which carried them into the hopper of the grinder intake. The fish, most measuring less than 12 inches long going into the machine, came out of the grinder as a thick chunky slurry, rich smelling and with an oily texture. This ground bunker chum would flow like thick stinky lava into a 4-foot square steel box with a sliding sluice gate on one side to allow it to fill the 5-gallon chum cans slid beneath it.

The chum cans were repurposed steel-coated industrial food ingredient containers obtained from the nearby Entenmann's bakery plant. The residual, often sugary remains in these cans attracted great swarms of yellow jacket bees which often got mixed into the chum. As the chum cans were filled, they were stacked on pallets, then layered three high using special wooden spreaders. Then an electric forklift stowed them in the aisles of the blast freezer.

Bunker chum hopper.

Because of their high oil content, bunkers made the best chum. Frozen chum was hung over the stern of a fishing boat and, as it slowly dissolved, the bits and pieces, and especially the oil, would attract small bait fish—which would in turn bring in the game fish being sought.

One year when bunkers were scarce and demand for chum was high, there was a particularly big run of albacore tuna. There was not much food demand for their red oily flesh, so my dad thought they would try to make chum out of them. The first problem was that the albacore were large fish—most around 2 feet long—and they were round and slippery. When put on a conveyor belt, they slipped right over the 2-inch-high rubber paddles on the belt, where they looked like they were swimming as they bounced over each paddle. So, they had to be placed in baskets and handed up to the grinder hopper one fish at a time. No Dutchman had the patience for that!

My dad had an idea! Bring out the Creasy Ice Breaker, another cast iron behemoth that had huge 6-inch spikes set in an 18-inch diameter rotating drum. 300-pound blocks of ice would be ice-picked into 25-pound chunks that were tossed with ice tongs into the maw of this noisy vibrating machine which shot the ice out as fist size chunks. Because they melted slower than the flaked ice, the chunks were preferred by the trawlers who stayed out at sea for days at time.

The plan was to feed the albacore into the Creasy Ice Breaker to bring them down to smaller sized chunks that would work more easily with the conveyor leading them into the grinder. Well … we tossed a few albacores into the ice machine—and chunks flew everywhere! The spikes grabbed the tough skin which stayed on as they spun madly around and flung fish flesh over everyone and everything within 20 feet. It had been a good idea … but ultimately was a failure.

With the continued demand for chum, it was back to feeding albacore into the grinder one football sized fish at a time. But fishermen complained that albacore wasn't oily enough to make a good chum. So Sunrise purchased tins of commercial bunker oil which was added to enhance the albacore chum. (Then there was the time when my brother Bob mistakenly mixed bunker oil instead of outboard motor oil with the gasoline for Dad's 2 stroke Evinrude outboard motor. The engine ran fine … but the exhaust smelled like bunkers!)

Setting Leaders

Squid

There were always a few squid in every catch, but sometimes there were thousands of pounds in the nets. When the pocket was being webbed up, the water would turn black from squid ink being ejected in their efforts to flee. As they were crowded together for the scoop net, the sharpie crew would be continually squirted with jets of water or black ink. Even as they were airborne in the scoop net, squid ink shot great distances, covering everyone.

As a kid, I recall curiously playing with a freshly landed squid, letting its tentacles suction to my hand and arm … until I felt a searing bite and shook the suction cups loose! My hand was bleeding from a painful nasty notch in my palm. Looking carefully at a dead squid, you can see the sharp parrot-like beak jaws of its mouth where the tentacles meet the body. No, I never did that again … but ask my brother Bob about the time he decided to pretend kiss the chomping buck-teeth lips of a blowfish!

Squid were typically iced down in barrels or down in the hold. As most of our market for these was for bait, they were sent off the boat in baskets and dumped with ice into large (4-foot-wide, by 4-foot-deep, by 8-foot-long) aluminum tanks on wheels. Galvanized steel tables were set up and the squid were netted out of the tank and piled onto the tables. There, several of us spent untold hours hand packing squid into one-pound black boxes. The flat boxes had to be opened up, several squid packed inside, the top of the box flapped down, the sides tucked in, and the box stacked in a tray for freezing. If we had 8,000 pounds of squid, we had to pack 8,000 individual boxes! There are more pleasant jobs than spending hours up to your elbows in dead squid juice and ink.

Sea Robin

While most fishermen consider the lowly sea robin a pest or trash fish, there can be a market for every species. The pound traps sometimes got several hundred pounds of sea robins. With them heaped up on deck, one had to be wary of their sharp dorsal spines which could easily puncture a boot … and the foot inside.

Sea robins were packed in waxed cardboard trays and frozen. Fish processing plants would purchase these for fish meal and pet food. The old pound boat actually had an opening door in the stern to more easily shovel overboard these and other "trash" fish. But later, when markets were found for most species, the new pound boat was designed without such a door.

As the pound trap was stationary, there was a wide variety in the species of fish caught. In addition to those mentioned above, they also caught herring, ling, cod, shad, bonito, dog fish, butterfish, angler (monkfish), skates, stingrays, and an occasional electric ray (which could give a jolt through a wire basket), various types of eels, various species of sharks (including thresher sharks, whose extended tails were as long as their bodies), mako sharks (which had great food value), sand sharks, fierce looking hammer head sharks, and blue sharks.

Some fish, like bluefish, tuna, and some species of shark, would be gutted or cleaned right away aboard the boat and then iced down. Someone who has not grown up with this might be a bit squeamish seeing a fisherman grab a live flapping fish, slit its belly open with a knife, grasp its entrails with his left hand while the knife in his right hand cut above the stomach by the head, quickly slice the back of the body cavity, and then throw the guts to a waiting gull while sliding the fish into the icy hold. An expert like Ward could dispatch a fish like this in less than five seconds!

With a good run of blues, there were thousands of fish to be gutted, keeping six crew busy. The men would occasionally pause to take a few swipes on a sharpening stone to keep their knife blades razor sharp. Each pair of workers shared a wooden bucket to toss the fish guts into, which took less time than tossing them overboard.

As a kid, it was my job to bring the men the sharpening stone and to empty the bucket of guts overboard. The bucket attracted the seagulls which would swarm about the boat, squawking and crying for the next morsel. They watched as I dragged the heavy bucket of bloody, delicious viscera to the gunwale. Bold birds would be literally in my face as they tried to pluck at the contents of the bucket before it could be dumped over the side. Occasionally a crewman would grab a flying gull and toss it below decks where the bird would calmly look about, wondering how it got there. (They would later be set free.) The brimming bucket of guts dumped over the side set off a flurry of screaming gulls and flashing wings, with birds having a tug of war with entrails strung out between their beaks pulling at the feast.

Ever curious, we would sometimes hold a still beating pink bluefish heart in the palm of our hands. The little heart would pulse and throb … then slow … until touched with a finger it would beat just a bit more before expiring. Then it would be tossed overboard … only to be plucked from the air by a hungry seagull. No, it wasn't gross—it was educational. Just like slicing open a large shark whose stomach contents revealed what it had been eating, and even sometimes seeing a dozen or more squirming 10-inch-long baby sharks, still connected to an egg sack, spill out of a female.

With tuna, we would closely examine the eyes. Big tuna swim deep in the ocean seeking squid and other prey in the dimly lit depths. So, like other species of the deep, such as squid and swordfish, their eyes have evolved as very large orbs to better gather the faint light. Bob and I once removed the entire eyeball from the head of a 900-pound tuna. It was the size of a softball. The clear covering of the eye was very tough, but yielded to a sharp knife. Further dissection drained the vitreous humor and we removed the perfectly clear marble-sized lens sphere. The view through the lens was clear but showed an inverted image. The back lining of the eyeball was the black surface of the retina. So, this was not gross to a ten-year-old—it was fascinating information.

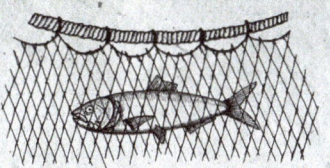

A Day in The Life of a Beach Kid

Some mornings started early … if they were arranged the night before: *'Dad? Is it gonna be a good weather day tomorrow for me to go fishing?'* When my brothers and sisters and I were quite young—too young to be actually working and helping on the pound boat—we would often go with my dad and crew into the ocean to raise the traps. Sometimes my mom even came.

Robin, Mom and Dad on an early morning trip on the pound boat.

We tried to not be in the way and help when we could. Every trip was a learning experience; how to properly tie knots, feeling the roll of the boat to get your sea legs, learning to differentiate between the many species of fish … and which ones to be careful of. Flapping, jumping bluefish on the deck could rip a piece out of a hand with their snapping razor sharp teeth. The spines on a sea robin could puncture right through a rubber boot into your foot. The slashing tail of a stingray could rip the skin off your arm or stab you with a slime covered barb. Sharks landing on deck slapped their tails and snapped their jaws viciously. Sometimes the fish on deck would be 18 inches deep. Wire baskets were spread out for "picking." That is, the crew would select and separate the species of fish into the baskets before icing and stowing them down certain hatches. If one of these baskets was placed on top of an electric ray and you grabbed the basket, you could get quite a shocking jolt! The electric ray sends out pulses of electric current to stun its prey before eating them. With a pile of fish on top of them on the deck, you could see a circular area of fish jump when a ray sent out a jolt.

We were always interested in the "by catch," the unusual fish not destined for market. Sometimes there were sea turtles in the nets—some incredibly big, like 6-foot-long leatherbacks. The crew would help them to freedom over the topline of the net. I recall bringing one-foot diameter green turtles back to the island. There we would hold the backs of their shells and swim with them before eventually releasing them.

Sometimes we would see threadfish swimming in the net; a thin silvery fish with a 6-inch-long body trailing 6-foot-long silver/white threads from its upper and lower fins. There were lookdowns; another silvery 5-inch fish, with eyes facing downward. Monk or angler fish came aboard, with their huge mouths open, and had to be shaken to empty the fish out of them. Despite their monster-like looks, when cleaned, the tail part of this fish is excellent eating—some liken it to lobster meat.

Monk or angler fish.

Setting Leaders

Now on the days that we did not get up early to go with Dad on the pound boat, we usually slept a little bit later. But not too late—the summer sun was up early, shining in the windows. The sounds of seagulls screeching, boats going by and waves washing on the shore gave promise to another glorious day of fun at the beach. Getting dressed was just a matter of slipping on one of several bathing suits—no shirts—no shoes. Mom would always have a great breakfast; blueberry pancakes were a favorite. Posted on the refrigerator was the chores list with each of the kids' names, the day of the week and a particular job: wash the dishes, dry the dishes, make your bed, help with the laundry, etc. After the chores, we were off to our adventures.

Beach kids in their element.

First adventure: down the dock to check the eel traps. We had several of these wire mesh traps that we baited with horseshoe crabs, bunkers, or crushed spider or green crabs. Our traps looked similar to this, but were homemade with wooden frames on the ends and a door hinged with leather or rubber on one end to empty out the catch.

    The eels were put in a bucket and then emptied into a floating "eel car." The eel car was a wooden box about 2 feet by 4 feet and about 10 inches deep with galvanized wire ends and bottom and a hatch on top to access the inside. The floating car would store the eels alive until we had enough to clean and eat, or sell. Since we got more money per pound for cleaned eels than whole ones, we usually cleaned them. Eels are slimy. To clean an eel, you had to first get a good grip on the slippery slimy writhing creature. We found it was easiest to do this up in the dry beach sand with several rags. The rags and sand helped get a grip on the eel while a long cut was made down its belly with a sharp knife. (The eels did not like this.) After the underside of the eel was cut open, the stomach and entrails were cut out. Then the underside of the head would be cut, but not all the way through—it was important to leave a bit of skin attached so as the head was pulled back, the remaining skin was removed by sort of turning it inside out. The cleaned eels were not at all slimy and had a nice bluish color to them. We wrapped them up in newspaper and iced them down for the trip into Islip on the pound boat to be sold to the Sunrise.

    Next, we would inspect all of the dock pilings for blue claw crabs. We were quite adept at catching crabs with our "scap nets." Sometimes there would be a "double." A larger crab would hold a smaller one under it until it sheds or molts. The shedder, or "peeler," as they call them in the Chesapeake, has a multicolored rainbow-like pattern on the flap on the bottom of its shell. We had other cars for holding shedders. These had to be checked frequently because once a crab sheds, it is vulnerable to being eaten by other crabs.

This crab shows the darkening on the triangular patch indicating it is ready to shed.

There were times we would catch a crab just as it was beginning to shed. We placed it in a bucket of seawater and watched the process. First the back of the shell began to open and the crab slowly withdrew its legs and claws from the shell. The crab seemed to back out of its shell and then just sit still—it must be an exhausting process. The "new" crab was maybe 20% bigger than the shell it crawled out of and was now called a soft crab. The shell, legs and claws were soft and rubber-like—we called it "like puddin'."

We would then take the newly shredded crab to Dad—and he would offer 25 cents for it; then to uncle Arie—who offered 30 cents; then back to Dad. A puddin' soft crab commanded top dollar!

Low tide offered the best time to go swimming, with the warm water flowing out from the shallow meadows and the bay. It was also best for clamming on the flats and for beachcombing, with the sand beach being at its widest for walking around the island. Daily strolls around the island yielded stray fishing dobbers (always in demand for snapper fishing), sometimes a bottle with a note inside, an occasional fishing float and a few tobacco pipes. My brother Bob and I would take the tobacco pipes home, boil them in water to sanitize them, and then fill the bowl with flour. It was fun to see Aunt Kate's reaction as we walked past her house puffing clouds of flour "smoke" from our pipes!

By noontime Mom expected us home for lunch. We often brought home a string of snappers or a few fresh eels that she fried up in the big cast iron skillet. We always liked to watch the fresh eels wiggle in the frying pan as they cooked. How many kids get to see that?

After lunch was mandatory nap time. We were told that if we swam right after eating, we would get cramps and drown … and that if we didn't rest in the early afternoon, we could get polio! (Mom's wisdom also imparted: *'Thunder is just the sound of two clouds bumping together',* and *'The steeple is where they put misbehaving boys in church.'*) Only recently did Mom admit that our nap time was about the only time she got a break since making my dad's breakfast before 6 a.m.

After nap time we were back at it; full speed ahead with swimming, playing in the boats, more fishing and crabbing. We also had a fleet of toy boats. Most of them we had made from scraps of wood, adding masts and booms to mimic the fishing boats. We played with these in the sand, forming docks and bridges and pretend islands.

When the dreaded summer day came that my parents hosted a huge family church group at the beach with hordes of little kids, I made a sign that said *'Don't touch my boats!'* My brother Bob laughed and said, "That won't work. Those little kids can't read!"

Decades before I climbed the 155-foot-high mast to furl the topgallant sails mid-Atlantic in a clipper ship, I got my training in a crow's nest that my dad built for us. He fitted a cut off 55-gallon drum to a stout pole set 6 feet in the sand and rigged ratlines to galvanized wire shrouds. It was topped with a flagpole topmast and crosstrees with flag halyards. Using her foot treadle Singer sewing machine, Mom made up signal flags spelling out *'Schapers are home'.* The view from the crow's nest was great … and it was where we could get our first glimpse of the pound boat returning from the ocean.

Setting Leaders

The crow's nest with Fire Island Lighthouse in the distance.

Chopped up horseshoe crabs were the preferred bait for killie and eel traps. The local bait station, Willie's, would pay us 25 cents apiece for female horseshoe crabs. Willie had a huge horseshoe crab pen under his dock at Captree Island, but he always needed more to keep his killie traps baited. During the early summer full moon, when the tide was the highest, the horseshoe crabs crawled ashore in massive numbers to spawn. Each large female had a smaller male crab attached to the back of her shell. With her legs, she would dig a bit of a hole in the sand at the high-water mark where she would deposit thousands of BB-size eggs which were then fertilized by the male.

This monthly congregation made it easy for us to drag a sharpie along in the shallow water off of Fire Island, grab the horseshoe crabs by their tails and load up with maybe a hundred crabs. We towed the sharpie behind our outboard powered garvey over to Willie's house on Captree Island to unload and count the crabs as we splashed them into his horseshoe pen.

It almost seemed like a rite of passage for my brothers and me to work at the bait dock. The oldest bait dock around was the Westbrook dock clinging to the edge of a small marshy island directly across from the Captree Boat Basin. The Westbrook family had built a small family compound on this island, with their white clapboard house perched upon locust poles. It contained a couple of bedrooms and an open kitchen/living room that also served as their office. The house was surrounded by an elevated deck which connected to several smaller sheds and to various boardwalks linked to the multilevel docks and buildings. The sheds by the house contained diesel generators, freezers and refrigerators. Facing along the State Boat Channel, the main dock was about 150 feet long. It was supported by thin flexible poles, faced with plywood, and laced with old fire hose for boat fenders. The dock swayed with the wakes of passing large boats. On the dock, a couple of small sheds housed large chest freezers holding chum cans, butter fish, bunkers, spearing, squid and clams.

There was a unique outhouse situated on the dock. This two-seater had a sheet copper funnel arrangement under the toilet seats to diminish breezy updrafts since they opened directly to the State Boat Channel flowing below. There was never a clog in this system and it included a stack of Playboy magazines, quite an education for a young teen!

The dock had an 8 foot by 10 foot "well" where a wire mesh screened pen held thousands of killies. These little fish were the mainstay of the bait business. They were used to bait thousands of hooks fishing for fluke, flounder, striped bass, blackfish and other species. The killies were sold live by the quart. A long-handled net was used to scoop into the killie pen to gather the fish and then the net full of killies was poured into a graduated aluminum pitcher over a wooden butter tub to catch the spilled-out fish. (A "buddah tub" or butter tub, was a wooden drum about 2 feet in diameter and 16 inches deep that was heavily fiberglassed inside and out for strength and to make it waterproof.) The measured volume of killies was transferred to the customers' buckets or killie cars.

The busiest time of day was early in the morning when the Captree boats would sail. As these party boats approached the bait dock, they would signal with their horns or loudspeakers how many quarts of killies and how many boxes of frozen squid they wanted. The baitman would frantically scoop and measure killies while my brothers and I would dig the squid out from the freezer. Each high-bowed party boat would maneuver close to the dock where the mate would lower a big bucket down for us to fill with bait. Then that boat backed off while the next in line moved in with his order. The party boats typically sailed at 7, 8 and 9 a.m., making those times extra busy. As these commercial boats had accounts, we didn't have to deal with taking payments and making change.

After the morning rush, the baitman would leave the dock to his assistants, one of my brothers or me, as he headed out in his boats to catch more killies and shiners.

The old boats used by the Westbrooks we referred to as bait barges. They were shaped like a garvey with a flat bottom and a swept up squared off bow. Nearly 30 feet long, these heavily built wooden boats had a large open working area for killie cars and traps, butter tubs, seine nets and horse shoe crab bait. They were each powered by a big inboard gasoline engine coupled to a propeller tucked up in a tunnel to allow them to traverse shallow waters. The slightly muffled dry exhaust shot straight in the air above the engine box. Steering was with a vertical stick; push forward to turn to starboard, pull back to turn to port. The Westbrook's boats were always painted a deep Kelly green. Like all baitmen's boats, they had a rich stinking aroma of rotten fish, bunker chum, horseshoe crab guts and gasoline.

The baitmen spent their days chopping up horseshoe crabs to bait their killie traps and placing the traps in the various coves and waterways that laced throughout the salt marshes. The horseshoe crabs were chopped up in a guillotine-like device with a curved cutting blade welded to an 18-inch-long handle. The crabs would be sliced once fore and aft, and once crossways, providing four parts, one part in each trap. After an overnight "soak," they would pull the traps, empty the killies into the heavy wood and galvanized mesh killie cars, re-bait the trap and move on. After these rounds, they would head back to the dock and secure the filled killie cars to pilings and replenish the big killie pen on the dock, as needed.

In between making repairs to docks and machinery, and maybe a bite to eat, they would be off again to seine for shiners. They always had favorite spots to find schools of shiners—usually along a sandy beach shore. Observing the water for signs of shiners, they would beach and anchor the boat. With a chunk of horseshoe crab or a tin of sardines, they put out a chum slick that would be carried by the current. The seine net was about 100 feet long and 4 feet high with ¼ inch mesh. It had cork floats every 4 feet along the top line and lead weights spaced along the lower side to hold it near the bottom. A small Danforth anchor was dug in on shore to hold one end of the net while the baitman, with chest high rubber waders, dragged the other end of the net offshore to surround his chum stream. He worked his way along the beach and then circled back in-shore to the anchored end of the net. With a well-practiced hauling on the lead line, balanced with pulling on the top float line so that captured fish did not swim over the net or scoot under it, the net was hauled up onto the sand. The big U-shaped net rippled with a bulge of excited fish. As the net was drawn together, the lead line bottom of the net was flipped into the butter tub and rolled over, dumping the catch of thousands of writhing, flapping silvery shiners into it. From a cooler, the baitman would grab a couple of blocks of ice to set in with the fish to keep them fresh. The net was pulled out straight, any seaweed or debris was shaken out, and it was rolled up and stowed in the boat. Back at the bait dock, the shiners were packed in small clear plastic bags and put in the freezer.

A seine net.

In later years, the Westbrooks sold the business to the much younger ... and wilder ... Gene Sweda. As all watermen must be, he was a hard worker. Even at my tender age, I could tell that he also partied hard. He was known to spend some late nights over at Fire Island ... and was really dragging when it came time to service the 7 a.m. party boats.

Gene had seen airboats in Florida ... and decided that was just what was needed in our thin waters. He apparently didn't calculate that, in the late afternoon, south westerlies kicked up a nasty chop against the tide. Making a sharp turn in his airboat in that chop sent him and his passengers into the water while the boat went to the bottom.

Around this time, the Lofstads, who had been supplying Westbrook's with bait, decided to set up their own bait dock. The father, Willie, spent his days catching bait in his 20-foot sharpie with an ancient 18 horsepower Johnson outboard in a well. That motor had a distinctive whine to it. Willie called it *Singing Lizzy*. Willie's Bait Dock was a stand-alone dock, not connected to any land, placed over near our island. The dock was about 50 feet long, faced with plywood, protected by fire hose and tire fenders, and supported by modest four to six-inch diameter tree trunks pumped into the sandy bottom in about 8 feet of water. Wave action in the channel made the dock sway as it was not anchored to any island as was Westbrook's. The thin poles were strong but flexible. People prone to sea sickness did not do well on this dock. Willie's was set up much like the other bait dock, with a small shed containing a couple of chest freezers for chum and frozen bait. A small generator was housed in a protective covering at the far end of the dock. In the center of the dock, down a couple of steps, was the large killie pen. We would sometimes swim in the pen with the killies just to feel the tickly sensation of being surrounded by thousands of little fish.

There were all kinds of ways island kids could earn a few dollars. Take the Wa Wa Yanda Club for instance. This was a popular sportsmen's club on the east end of Captree Island. It was built in 1860 when these islands were still fairly remote. Boat service from the mainland brought wealthy men out for hunting and sport fishing. There was a two-story hotel with a restaurant and bar. A long dock extended into the bay to accommodate ferries and freight boats. Most of the facilities were destroyed in the famous 1938 hurricane, and there was a fire in the early 1950s that left only a portion of the original structures standing. A renovation in the early 1960s turned it into a funky bar and restaurant. That's the era I recall.

As an off-the-grid restaurant and bar, it had to run a generator full time. Out fifty feet beyond the back of the kitchen was a rickety old shed housing an even more dilapidated ancient diesel generator that ran 24/7 to keep the refrigerators and freezers working. The fuel for this generator had to be hauled in by hand in 5-gallon jerry cans. That was one of my jobs. Using the restaurant owner's garvey, I loaded the boat with 15-20 empty jerry cans, brought the boat to the Captree fuel dock and filled up. Now these were not the nice red plastic jerry cans from Home Depot. These were all repurposed, cylindrical, rusty, dented, steel lube oil cans in various stages of decay. Most had screw-on caps on the spouts. Some were "sealed" with a dirty rag. After filling the cans with diesel fuel, I motored slowly back to the Wa Wa Yanda Club dock to unload.

Lifting the 40-pound rag-sealed cans over my head up to the dock from the boat was … messy. Then, the cans had to be lugged down the dock, along a sandy path lined with poison ivy, past the restaurant/bar and the kitchen, back to the generator shed. The sand around the shed was soaked with black oil and spilled diesel fuel, choking off the weeds around its perimeter. The walls and floor of the generator shed were charred from some previous fires and were liberally coated with soot and black dirty lube oil. The generator itself was a venerable 71 series Detroit Diesel with faded green paint, oozing with leaking oil and steaming vapors. The sight of this filthy machine was all the more shocking to me as I was used to the nearly pristine condition of my dad's boat engines. To me, it was amazing that such a neglected engine could run so reliably and produce the essential electricity to run this operation. Outside the shed was a rusty horizontal cylindrical steel fuel tank that held about 250 gallons of diesel. Each jerry can had to be lifted 5 feet off the ground in order to empty it into a corroded steel funnel to fill the tank. I was paid a few dollars per jerry can. No wonder the owner didn't want to do it himself.

The Wa Wa Yanda Club can be seen in the distance in the upper left of this photo of Captain Wayne Westerlind navigating the State Boat Channel as he was approaching the Captree Boat Basin. This likely dates from the early 1960s.

While the proprietors were promoting the restaurant at the Wa Wa Yanda Club, they somehow gathered up a few busloads of people, enticing them with an exotic dinner outing. My dad was pressed into service with the pound boat to transport the people from Captree Boat Basin and deliver them to the club. Folding chairs and wooden benches were set up on the closed hatches for the passengers. We, of course, were used to the fishy aroma of the pound boat … but these folks soon found out this was no luxury cruise. (My dad always used to say, "That's not the smell of fish … that's the smell of money!") Fortunately, there were no incidents. And while Dad made a few dollars and got a meal out of it, I'm not sure what his insurance company or the US Coast Guard would have said about using the fishing boat as a ferry.

The restaurant at the Wa Wa Yanda Club didn't last too long before it finally shut down for good. Even before it had been renovated, there had been a long-time caretaker of the property who lived by himself year-round in a small shack just west of the club. His name was Elijah Raynor. Everyone called him Liege. He was the definition of a hermit. Liege used a hand rake to dig clams in the shallow cove by the club. Periodically, my dad took the skiff over to the flats near Liege's shack and he would take his clams into market. In return, Dad would bring Liege food and staples: rice, potatoes, onions, vegetables, canned foods, and whiskey.

Elijah (Liege) Raynor

Setting Leaders

This painting of Liege was by a local artist. As I recall, his name was Mellon.

All the beach kids were afraid of Liege. He was "creepy." My brothers and I knew that my dad dealt with him. I had even accompanied Dad in the skiff a couple of times to get Liege's clams or to give him his groceries. He was a tall man. Living as he did, he was weathered looking and wore old, dirty, long khaki trousers and long-sleeved shirts, with a wide-brimmed cloth hat. As a kid, it was hard to determine an adult's age, but he was a lot older than my dad. He looked ancient.

One time, when my brothers and I were on the shore near the deserted Wa Wa Yanda Club, we noticed his shack and decided to pay him a visit! It wasn't my idea. I was scared. But there we were—we called out "Hello! Liege?" The door of the weather-beaten shack creaked open. The surprised look on his wrinkled face turned to an almost smile as we told him we were "Louie's kids." He invited us in! The small room had a single bed on one side and a tiny kitchen set up on the other side. Canned goods and boxed foods were stacked on wall shelves. Most notable to a young kid were a couple of Playboy magazine pinups on the wall. After a brief chat, we were back to our boat with a new understanding of hermit Liege of Captree Island.

Spending as much time as we did in the water, it was only natural that we wanted to explore under water. Starting with a simple mask, snorkel and flippers, we lashed dinner forks (sorry Mom) to broom sticks to spear eels, flounders or anything else in range. Dad also shared our enthusiasm for diving which was brought to another level by his friendship with Artie Jutner, a professional diver with the police department. With his guidance, we learned the technical aspects of scuba diving.

Robin shows that we started diving at an early age.

When we were living at the beach in the summer, we hated having to go ashore to the mainland. But every Sunday we had to go to Babylon to go to church. While we didn't like having to leave the beach, after church we began to make regular visits to the Babylon Sport Shop for more diving equipment. That made going ashore on Sundays a lot more enjoyable! Diving is a very equipment intensive sport. Over the years, we added to and upgraded all of our diving gear—which eventually included a few dive tanks and regulators. Dad even got a wetsuit.

My first aqualung dive experience, however, was at the tender age of 11 … with no training. It was at the old Westbrook's Bait Dock. Gene, the new owner/baitman, had a dive tank with a full-face mask regulator. When I showed interest in it, he strapped it on my back, snapped the mask on my face and put me overboard in the State Boat Channel. I was too excited to be breathing underwater for the first time to be scared of the boats buzzing along nearby.

Along with occasional ocean dives at and in the fish traps, weather permitting, we would dive on something called the *Roda* wreck. This was a 315-foot British coal-fired steamship with a cargo of copper ore that sank off of Cedar Beach in 1908. While most of the vessel had disappeared, the steering quadrant was just barely visible above water. We were able to spear a few good-sized striped bass and blackfish there and my brother Richard found a brass ship's telegraph handle.

A favorite spear fishing dive was drifting along with the current by the Fire Island Inlet rock jetty. We would secure our boat at the inshore end of the jetty, build a little campfire of driftwood, then go into the typically cold water—without the luxury of wetsuits. Using pole spears or Hawaiian slings, we hunted flounders and blackfish, and sometimes we could pull lobsters from the rocks. By the time we got back to the boat, the campfire had died down to coals. We would clean the fish and mount them on driftwood boards next to the glowing embers. Lobsters were combined with a few black mussels, wrapped in wet seaweed and placed in the fire to steam. Forty-five minutes or so later, we had a succulent feast fresh from the ocean.

Another favorite spot in the inlet was an underwater ledge so reliable for producing fish that we called it "the fish market." Once Richard speared a huge fluke there that was so big that, when we weighed it at Captree, he was encouraged to enter it in a fishing contest. When he said that he had speared it, not caught it with a fishing pole, they said, "you don't have to tell them that!" No, he did not falsely enter it.

Some special evenings after dinner, Dad would load us all in the skiff and take us over to Fire Island. It was called Fire Island State Park back then (after the bridge was built over the inlet, it was renamed Robert Moses State Park) and public access was by several ferries that operated from Captree Boat Basin. We knew the names and characteristics of all of the ferries and we each had our favorites, even though we never ever rode on one. When we were swimming by the jetty, we enjoyed riding the big wakes the ferries left as they streamed by the island. The kids would yell out *'Waves! waves! waves!'* as we splashed with our floats and rafts.

These ferries only ran during the day. In fact, Fire Island State Park was officially closed at night. Fortunately, my dad knew "the official" who managed the park, so it was okay for us to go there after hours. We would dock in the boat basin and walk across to the ocean. Our bare feet were not used to walking on concrete sidewalks which were still warm from the sun. We would shout out to hear echoes as we passed through the concrete tunnel that ran under the road providing access to the ocean beach. The pavilion was closed and we were the only people there. We raced to see which kid would be the first to dive in the ocean waves. After a great romp in the surf, it was time to head home. To our delight, hoppy toads and rabbits would be out, enjoying the quiet evening. Back in the skiff, bundled in beach towels against the cool night air, we would squeeze into the tiny forward cabin for warmth.

A few times each summer, in the evening, the old wooden ice cream churn would be brought out on the front porch of the house. When we had an abundance of fresh peaches, Mom would cut them up and mix them with condensed milk, sugar and other delicious ingredients, put them in the 2-quart metal container, then insert the top with the wooden paddles. The crank mechanism was clamped on and flaked ice from the pound boat was packed around the cylinder. Alternate layers of ice and coarse salt were replenished as the ice melted and drained out an upper drain hole. All of the kids took turns cranking the handle, churning the ice cream. After an interminable amount of time, the churning was halted and the container was opened—but first it had to go into the freezer for a while. We initially had to be content with just licking the paddles. Finally, the finished product was brought out of the freezer, doled out into bowls and the supremely delicious homemade peach ice cream was served! Somehow though, a bit of the salt always found its way into the ice cream … but nobody complained.

Setting Leaders

Late in the summer, the wild blackberries were ripe and ready for picking! While we were used to wearing only bathing suits, in order to go blackberry picking we had to put on long-sleeved shirts and long pants tucked into socks and shoes for protection. The blackberry bushes were armed with sharp thorns and they grew interspersed with virulent poison ivy. We would gather Mom's larger pots and pans, buckets and pails to collect the berries. The back of the island, where the blackberry bushes grew, was out of the refreshing breezes so it made it hot and there was often an active mosquito population. Wading into the bushes, we worked quickly and soon had many quarts of berries. Afterward, Mom insisted that we scrub down with her nasty yellow lye soap to remove the poison ivy oils. It wasn't pleasant, but it usually seemed to work.

Back in the kitchen, aside from eating the blackberries whole and ungarnished, we enjoyed mouthwatering blackberry pancakes, and the whole house would take on the heavenly aroma of Mom making blackberry jam and pies. Many wax-covered jars of jam were put away for the winter.

On still summer nights when the breeze was light, the calm water was glassy and perfect for "jacking." Bright Coleman gas lamps were rigged on the bow of a garvey with reflectors directing the bright light into the water ahead of the boat. Quietly poling along in the shallows, the lights revealed eels and crabs, sometimes fluke or flounders, out foraging in the dark. The light would seem to stun them, making it easier to spear them or to scoop them up with a net. In fact, there was a commercial fisherman using this method in the Fire Island Inlet who sold his catch of large fluke and striped bass to the Sunrise. The man was a skilled professional, spearing all of his prey in the head, not leaving any marks on the body flesh.

At least once a week, usually on a Saturday night, despite being in and out of the water all day, we kids needed a bath. Mom's largest galvanized wash tub was put in the middle of the kitchen floor. Several pots of water were heated on top of the stove, then poured into the tub. Taking turns, one after the other, we had a bath and a good scrub down right there in the kitchen. The wash tub was left with a sediment of sand on the bottom and a scummy floating layer of dirty soap suds on the top. By then the lighthouse was on, so it was time for bed.

The waning days at the end of August were cloaked with the foreboding shadow of the ending of those golden times of summer. *'The summer couldn't be over already! We still have too much to do! We've got eel traps set and shedders in the car and the snappers are still running!'* How can kids adjust to being indoors in school all day when they are used to constantly moving and reveling in being outside and in and on the water? How can these barefoot kids be expected to cram their tough summer feet into shoes after being shoe-less for two months? *'We have to put our boats away for the winter? But it's sunny and 84 degrees! Pack up and load the skiff!? We just got here!'* Just like we had to go to bed when the lighthouse came on, it was time to say goodbye.

Goodbye big net shed.

Goodbye beach house.

Goodbye scow. Goodbye sharpies. Goodbye dock. Goodbye island.

This slice of life at the beach house and on the island is over for now. But the value of the time spent there, the many learning experiences; about boats and the sea—about life and people—about how to be independent and resourceful; that value runs deep and endures.

Storms come, the island erodes, buildings are moved or crumble into the bay. Many of the old fishermen have "crossed the bar"—but the next generation has been instilled with the call of the sea. They carry on the traditions, maybe not of the fishing, but of the value and beauty of life on the island. Now Pieter Schaper's great-great-grandchildren are learning the ways of beach kids. May their island days be ever rewarding and joyful.

The approach to the island, past the protective jetty, with the scow holding a net aloft to dry. This was always the first and last view of the island.

In Closing

A Fisherman's Wind Barometer

The wind blowing from the north causing kitchen curtains to billow doesn't mean much to most folks, but to a commercial fisherman it's a good sign that the men will 'have a day' in the ocean. The scow can roll, poles can be pumped, a dirty net can be changed or leaders set.

A south-east 'slop' is an almost sure omen of a swinging boatload of blues with the boat coming back filled to the gunnels.

A north-easter brings rain and wind - too stormy to raise the nets that day and maybe for a day or two thereafter. But with a dry north-easter, (though too rough as white caps churn up the bay) the crew can catch up on mending the holes that the bluefish chewed through the net, or untangle a section of leader jumbled up from the last storm.

The prevailing summer wind direction at the beach, south-west, brings a gentle cool breeze from the ocean and allows the fishermen easy access through the inlet and out to raise the trap.

The driest wind of all comes from the north-west. Not only does it hasten the nets drying on the dock but it actually flattens out the ocean like a mill pond, knocking down the waves and making it almost a pleasure to work with instead of against the elements.

The wind plays an integral part in a fisherman's life. The tops of the trees are scrutinized at dawn and at dusk - "Is it blowing?" - "Are the tree tops moving?" - "Does it seem to be blowing hard or gently?" "Where is it coming from?" The wind sets the tone. Will it be a good day or one of struggle?

Written by my mom, Mary Schaper, this piece was published in the September 2011 issue of National Fisherman magazine.

The arrow points to Fishermen's Island in New York's Great South Bay, near Fire Island Inlet and Captree State Park.

Fishermen's Island, also known as Havemeyer Point Island, is where the fish camps and beach houses were located.

www.ingramcontent.com/pod-product-compliance
Lightning Source LLC
Chambersburg PA
CBHW041723070526
44585CB00006B/133